How to write a report your boss will read and remember

How to write a report your boss will read and remember

RAYMOND V. LESIKAR

 1974

Dow Jones-Irwin, Inc.   Homewood, Illinois 60430

First Printing, July 1974

Printed in the United States of America

Library of Congress Cataloging in Publication Data
Lesikar, Raymond Vincent.
    How to write a report your boss will read and
remember

    1. Business report writing.   2. Report writing.
I. Title.
HF5719.L444   808'.066'65178021   74-10902
ISBN 0-87094-078-3

Preface

The goal of this book is to help you write better reports.

In my work as a business consultant, I have found executives disappointed with the reports their subordinates write. And rarely have I found a report writer who truly was satisfied with his abilities or his results. Business wants and needs better report writers. Hopefully, this book will make a contribution to this end.

At first glance, the idea that a single book will help you as well as the other report writers in business may appear to be overambitious. Reports are far from standardized; and practices vary widely. Close analysis, however, reveals that the differences are more imagined than real. They are more related to subject matter than to procedure. In fact, universal principles and procedures exist. In this book I have attempted to identify these principles and procedures and to make them meaningful to you.

If I have achieved my goal, this book should be useful to you whether you are an accountant, engineer, chemist, salesman, or whatever. For it to be most useful to you, you will need to focus your attention on the basic messages presented. You will need to avoid looking at the illustrations for their specific subject content. Rather, you will need to look at them for the principles and practices they illustrate. And you will need to adapt these principles and practices to the unique needs of your own situation.

In writing a book such as this one, I quite naturally had to draw on the work and experiences of others. Most significant are the

v

unknown writing practitioners who over the years have developed the subject matter I have assembled. More specifically, I am indebted to the report writers with whom I have worked in my consulting activities in business. Especially am I indebted to those report writers at Kaiser Aluminum and Chemical Corporation, Exxon Company, and Ethyl Corporation. Although I was hired to teach them, I learned much from them. I learned from talking report writing with them; and I learned from my analyses of the report specimens with which they so liberally supplied me. Much of what I learned is sprinkled throughout the book. And many of the illustrations used come from reports written by these most cooperative people.

At the scene of my work I am indebted to Gloria Armistead, my secretary, for her skillful work in transforming rough notes into finished manuscript. And for her love, understanding, and infinite capacity to put up with my after-hours work, I am indebted to my wife. As this is only one in what must appear to be an endless succession of writing projects for me, surely I have tested her patience to the limit. For this and other personal reasons, I dedicate this book to her.

June 1974   R. V. LESIKAR

Contents

formulas. The Gunning Fog Index. Critical appraisal of the formulas. The importance of objectivity: *Objectivity as a basis for believability. Objectivity and the question of impersonal versus personal writing.* Consistency in time viewpoint. Structural aids to report coherence: *The use of introductory, concluding, and summarizing sections. Communication value of transition.* The role of interest in report communication. Differences in short and long reports: *Less need for introductory material. Predominance of direct order. More personal writing style. Less need for coherence plan.*

transmittal and authorization. Acknowledgments. Table of contents. Table of illustrations.

9. Handling secondary information   161

Text use of secondary information. Construction of source footnotes: *When to footnote. Placement of the footnote. Variation in footnote makeup. Footnote form with a bibliography. Form of the footnote without a bibliography. Double sources. Standard reference forms. Discussion footnotes.* Makeup of the bibliography. Structure of the annotated bibliography.

1

Some introductory remarks

The goal of this book is to help you improve your report writing. If you are like most people in the business and professional world, writing is not easy for you. The chances are it is one of the most difficult tasks you must perform, and your skill at it is likely to be below your other work skills. Hopefully, this book will give you the help you need to improve this situation.

THREE VIEWPOINTS OF THE APPROACH

In an effort to achieve this goal, the following review of report writing instruction is arranged to support three basic viewpoints: (1) that report writing instruction should be practical, (2) that it should permit easy adaptation, and (3) that it should be communication oriented. As these three viewpoints describe the book's approach to the subject, a quick explanation of them should help your understanding and appreciation of the subject matter.

Emphasis on practical instruction

That the practical viewpoint should be used is consistent with the goal of this book. As the book's title clearly states, this is a how-to-do-it book. And by definition a how-to-do-it book is practical. In applying this viewpoint, the book avoids the theoretical and academic discussions typically found in books on writing. Likewise, it

1

avoids the sweeping generalities with which all of us would agree but which really do not show us how to write better reports. Instead, the book works to get right down to the gritty task of writing reports. Wherever possible, it uses realistic examples. In general, it does not just talk about writing; it shows you how to do it.

Provision for adaptation

The need to make the instruction adaptable to all report writing situations should be apparent. If you have had the opportunity to observe many of the reports written in business, you know that they vary greatly in format, organization, subject matter, writing style—in fact, in just about every way they could vary. Many of these variations, of course, are frivolous or downright illogical. But some fit the needs of the individual company. In fact, legitimate variations are sufficiently numerous to cause authorities to conclude that no one correct procedure exists for many areas of report writing.

In view of this confusing picture of reports, it is difficult to present specific instructional material that will be useful to all report writers in all situations. If this objective is to be met, in places the instruction must be broad—sufficiently broad to permit adaptation to any given situation. It must be adaptable to the needs of all types of organizations. It must be sufficiently flexible to be useful in reporting information ranging from the highly technical to the very general. It must fit the needs of all types of readers. The objective of this book is to do all this. But even though the instruction sometimes must be broad in its coverage, the plan is to show by example how the broad instruction may be applied in a given case.

Primary goal of communication

The third viewpoint which forms the approach of this book is that communication should be the primary goal of any business report. On first thought this statement may appear to be elementary and obvious. Certainly one might say that all writing has the goal to communicate. In some situations, however, writers bring in other goals; and these goals may interfere with the communication goal. For example, all too often a report writer feels that he must impress his reader with his words. How he writes becomes more important than what he writes. As a result, he clouds his message with sophisticated words and expressions. Or, for another example, a writer may feel that he should entertain with clever rhetoric, rhythmic structures, humorous illustrations, and such. As we shall point out emphatically in this book, such devices tend to work against the communication goal by detracting the reader's attention from the message. For reasons such as these, the instruction in the following pages stresses the goal of communicating—or, more precisely, of making certain that the message intended is the message received.

A LOGICAL ORDER OF PRESENTATION

Presentation of the instruction follows the order in which it occurs in a report writing situation. Thus, this review begins with the logical first step of organizing the information for the report. Next it covers the task of determining the form the report should take. A succession of chapters on writing follows, each covering a segment of the next step in the procedure. The book concludes with a coverage of the mechanics involved in putting the report into its final form. To illustrate the whole of the effort, a selection of illustration reports is appended to the book.

This order is ideal for those who wish to study the book from cover to cover. They merely start at the beginning and read to the end, applying their readings to their knowledge of report writing experience as they go along. But no doubt some users of the book will not need or want to follow this complete coverage. Their needs are for specific information here and there throughout the book. They are more likely to use the book as a reference source than as a text for thorough study. The book is planned to meet these readers' needs, also. As far as possible, each part is made independent of the other parts. You should be able to dip into the book at any part, quickly get your bearing, and get what you need. Hopefully, whatever your needs for report writing instruction, you should find them here.

A WORD OF CAUTION

As you move into this review of report writing instruction, a word of caution is in order. Do not expect miracles. Even though this instruction is designed to help you in the most practical way possible, it will not bring about improvement overnight. Any progress you make is apt to appear imperceptible; improvement will come only after long and hard effort. But that is the nature of the beast. Rest assured that you can improve your report writing. Countless others have done it. The materials for improvement are now before you. You have only to set your mind to the task of putting them in practice.

2

Determining the
report makeup

Our review of report writing instruction begins with the task of determining the makeup your report will have. Will it be a simple, informal memorandum? Will it be a long, formal paper? Or will it take one of a number of other possible forms? As you may know, reports differ widely in structure, so you will want to choose just the right one for your one case.

By beginning with report makeup, we skip over the research phase of your report work—a phase that may well be a major part of your work. Although your research may be the bulk of the work you do on a report, our goal in this book is to help you present, not find, information. Finding information (research methodology) is quite another subject, and it is well beyond the scope of this book. Anyway, the chances are that your past experience and training have equipped you to handle the research part. Your primary need is likely to be for help in presenting the findings.

AN OVERVIEW APPROACH
TO REPORT MAKEUP

Because the makeup of reports differs so much from company to company, it is most difficult to cover the subject logically. In view of this difficult situation, two plans for covering the subject matter appear as possibilities. One is to cover each of the many physical variations that exist—or at least the most common variations. The

5

other is to devise a broad and general coverage of the subject—that is, to take an overview of the subject, emphasizing the similarities and general practices among the variations. The first plan would be unworkable, for the variations we would need to cover are much too numerous. Thus, we shall take the second approach.

Structural relationships of all reports

Our overview approach to report makeup takes all the reports written and arranges them in stair-step fashion according to their formality and length (see Figure 2-1). At the top of this stairway are the most formal and longest reports. At the bottom are the most informal, shortest ones. And between these extremes are all the other reports. As we view the reports in this arrangement, we see that many variations still exist in their makeups, but we also see some similarities. We are able to make some general observations about these similarities which should guide you in finding appropriate makeups for the reports you write.

Inspection of the reports at the top of the stairway reveals that they cover the longer and more involved problems. Typically they concern somewhat formal situations. In addition to containing written presentations of the information gathered, these reports have a number of parts. These parts appear before the report text in much the same way that prefatory parts appear before the text material of most published books. Obviously, such parts are included mainly for reasons of formality and length, for they are in addition to the report message. Although there is no one standardized set of prefatory parts, these are the most common ones: title fly, title page, letter of transmittal, table of contents, and summary (also called synopsis, epitome, digest, précis). Detailed descriptions of the content and form of these parts appear elsewhere in this book.

As we move down this stairway illustration, the reports become shorter and less formal, and their makeup tends to change. Although these changes are far from standardized, they follow a general order. First, the somewhat useless title fly drops out. This page contains nothing other than the title, and the title information appears on the next page. Obviously, the page is used strictly for reasons of formality. Next in the progression, the synopsis (summary) and the transmittal letters are combined. When this stage is reached, the report problem usually is short enough to permit its summary in

FIGURE 2-1

Progression of change in report makeup as formality requirements and length of the problem decrease

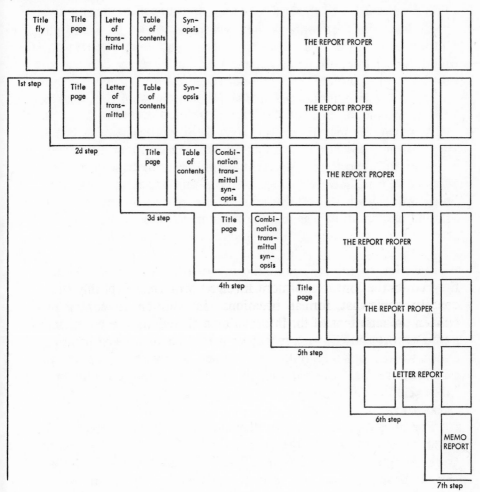

relatively short space. A third step down, the table of contents drops out. The table of contents is a guide to the report text, and such a guide serves little value in a short report. Certainly, a guide to a 100-page report is necessary, and a guide to a 1-page report is illogical. Somewhere between these extremes a dividing point exists. The report writer should follow the general guide of including a table of contents whenever it appears to be of some value to the reader.

Another step down as formality and length requirements continue to decrease, the combined letter of transmittal and synopsis drops out. Thus, the report now has only a title page and report text. The title page remains to the last because it serves as a very useful cover page. In addition, it contains the most important of the identifying information. Below this short-report form is a report that reinstates the letter of transmittal and summary and presents the entire report in the form of a letter—thus, the letter report. And finally, for short problems of even more informality the memorandum (informal letter) form may be used.

As previously mentioned, this analysis of report change is at best general, and perhaps it oversimplifies changes in report structure. Few of the reports actually written coincide exactly with its steps. Most of them, however, fit generally within the framework of the diagram. Knowledge of this relationship of length and formality should be helpful in planning the makeup of your report.

Elements of the formal report

In a sense, your task of designing a report is much like that of the architect. We are assuming, of course, that your employer permits a choice in report makeup. (Many do not.) Both you as the planner of a report and the architect have a number of possible elements with which to work. Both of you seek to select and arrange the elements to meet the requirements of a given situation. And to do this skillfully, both of you must know well the elements at your disposal.

For you, the report writer, these elements are the report parts. Starting at the top of the stairway with a typical formal report containing a full complement of prefatory parts, you may include them all, select those most appropriate, or alter them in various ways to build the one report that best fits your needs. You can even omit all report parts and use a memorandum or letter report—a type discussed later in the chapter.

The following outline of the parts of this traditional, long formal report serves as a preview to the discussion that follows. (Such a report is illustrated in Appendix A, and the mechanics of its parts are shown in Chapter 8.) For ease and understanding, the parts are arranged by groups. First are the prefatory parts—those that are most related to the formality and length of the report. Then comes the report proper, which, of course, is the meat of all reports. It is the report story. The parts before and after it are to some extent mainly trappings. The final group consists of appended parts. These contain supplementary materials. As a rule, these materials are not essential to the report presentation. They are included largely to serve any special interests the reader may have in the problem or to help the reader in his use of the report.

Prefatory parts:
    Title fly.
    Title page.
    Letter of transmittal, preface, or foreword.
    Table of contents and list of illustrations.
    Synopsis.
The report proper:
    Introduction.
    The report findings (usually presented in two or more major divisions).
    Conclusions, recommendations, or summaries.
Appended parts:
    Appendix.
    Bibliography.

Construction of the prefatory parts

Construction of the prefatory parts of a report is somewhat routine and mechanical. In some companies, precise arrangements for these pages are prescribed. As the following discussion illustrates, however, some room remains for the application of good logic and imagination.

Title fly. First among the possible parts preceding the report text is the title fly. Typically it contains only the report title, which it displays with eye-appealing balance (see page 176). A similar page appears in most books. Its usefulness is questionable, for, as we shall see, the title appears also on the following page, and probably also on the outside cover. Obviously, the page is included for formal and traditional reasons.

Title page. Like the title fly, the title page presents the report title. But it also displays other information essential to the identification of the report (see page 150). Usually, it presents the complete identification of the writer and the authorizer or recipient of the report. As we discussed earlier, this is the last of the prefatory parts to drop out as the report changes form. It remains to the last because the title page contains some valuable identification material and also because it can serve as a logical cover to a report.

Letter of transmittal. Most formal reports contain some form of personal communication from writer to reader. In most business cases, a letter of transmittal or a memorandum of transmittal makes this contact. In some formal cases, particularly when the report is addressed to a group of readers, a foreword or preface performs this function.

As its name implies, the letter of transmittal is a letter (or memorandum) that transmits the report to the intended reader. In addition, it makes whatever remarks the writer wishes to make to his reader about the report. And as we noted in our review of report structure, sometimes it contains a summary of findings. Typically, the letter begins with a direct transmittal of the report, without explanation or other delaying information. Thus, the opening words say, in effect, "Here is the report." Tied to or following this statement of transmittal usually comes a brief identification of the subject matter of the study and possibly an incidental summary reference to the authorization information (who assigned the report, when, etc.).

If the letter is combined with the synopsis, as may be done in some forms of reports, the opening transmittal and identification may be followed by a quick review of the report highlights, much in the manner described in the following discussion of the synopsis. But whether the letter of transmittal does or does not contain a synopsis of the report text, generally the writer uses the letter to make helpful and informative comments about the report. He may, for example, make suggestions about how the report information may be put to use. He may suggest follow-up studies, point out special limitations, or mention side issues of the problem. In fact, he may include anything that helps the reader to understand or appreciate the report.

Except in very formal instances, the letter affords the writer an opportunity to more or less chat with the reader. Such letters might well reflect the warmth and vigor of the writer's personality. Generally, good use of personal pronouns *(you, I, we)* is made. A warm note of appreciation for the assignment or a willingness and desire to further pursue the project traditionally marks the letter close.

Minor distinctions sometimes are drawn between forewords and prefaces, but for all practical purposes they are the same. Both are preliminary messages from writer to reader. Although usually they do not formally transmit the report, forewords and prefaces do many of the other things done by letters of transmittal. Like the letters of transmittal, they seek to help the reader appreciate and understand the report. They may, for example, include helpful comments about the report—its use, interpretation, follow-up, and such. In addition, prefaces and forewords frequently contain expressions of indebtedness to those helpful in the research. Like the letters of transmittal, they usually are written in first person, but seldom are they as informal as some letters. Arrangement of the contents of prefaces and forewords follows no established pattern.

Table of contents and list of illustrations. If a report is long enough for a guide to its contents to be helpful, it should have a table of contents. This table is the report outline in the finished, polished form we discuss in Chapter 3, with the addition of page numbers. If the report has a number of tables, charts, illustrations, and the like, a separate table of contents (see page 158) may be set up for them.

Synopsis. The synopsis (also called summary, abstract, digest, précis, epitome) is the report in miniature. It concisely summarizes all the essential information of the report. It includes all the major facts as well as the major analyses and conclusions derived from these facts. Primarily, it is designed for the busy reader who may not have time to read the whole report. But it is also a preview or review for those who very carefully read the entire report.

In constructing the synopsis, you simply reduce the parts of the report in order and in proportion. As your objective is to cut the report to a fraction of its length (usually less than one eighth), much of your success will be determined by your skill in directness and word economy. With space at a premium, loose writing is obviously costly. But in your efforts to achieve conciseness, you are likely to find your writing style dull. Thus, you must work hard to give this concise bit of writing a touch of color and style interest to reflect the tone of the main report.

Although most synopses simply present the report in normal order (normally from introduction to conclusion), there is some usage nowadays of a more direct opening (see Figure 2-2). Such a plan shifts the major findings, conclusions, or recommendations (as the case may be) to the major problem of emphasis at the beginning. From this direct beginning the summary moves to the introductory parts and thence through the report in normal order.

FIGURE 2-2
Diagram of the synopsis in normal order and in direct order

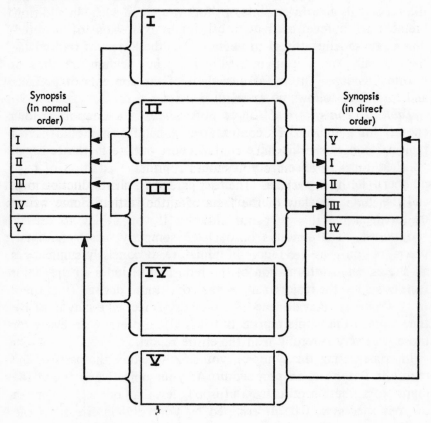

Content of the report proper

The main part of the report is the write-up of the information being presented. And, as we have noted, in some of the less formal, shorter reports, this part is the whole report. Because much of our concern about report writing involves this part, it is the subject of much of our discussion in the following chapters.

Your presentation of the report contents may follow any of a number of general arrangements. Most companies prefer the more conventional arrangements (direct, logical, chronological) discussed in Chapter 3. Some companies prefer to prescribe a definite arrangement for all reports, particularly for the technical ones. For examples of some of these variations, you may look at the reports presented in the Appendixes. As you will see, most of these variations are only rearrangements of the same general information. Thus, you should be able to adapt to other arrangements from the following review of the content of the body of a conventional logical-order report.

Introduction. The purpose of the introduction of the report is to orient the reader to the problem at hand. In this undertaking you may include scores of possible topics, for you may include anything which will help your reader to understand and appreciate the problem. Although the possible contents are varied, there are certain general topics of coverage you should consider.

1. Origin of the report. The first part of your introduction might well include a review of the facts of authorization. Some writers, however, leave this part out entirely. If you decide to use this section, you will present facts such as when, how, and by whom the report was authorized, who wrote the report, and when the report was submitted. This section is particularly useful in reports which have no letter of transmittal.

2. Purpose. A vital part of almost every report you will write is a description of the purpose of your investigation. Called by other names (objective, problem, object, aim, goal, mission, assignment, proposal, project, etc.), the purpose of the report is the value to be attained by the solving of the problem. It may be a long- or short-term value, or a combination of both.

You may state the purpose of your report in an infinitive phrase ("to propose standards of corporate annual reports"), or in the form of a well-phrased question ("What retail advertising practices do Centerville consumers disapprove of?"). Usually, you will need no more than a single sentence for this major purpose.

You will also need to state collateral, or secondary, purposes in this section. If a major problem is solved, collateral values are achieved. By stating these values, you help to convince the reader of the worthwhileness of your report. In other words, you should use a positive approach by telling what the solved problem can do for your reader.

3. Scope. If the scope of the problem is not clearly covered in any of the other introductory sections, you may need to include it in a separate section. By "scope," we mean the boundaries of the problem. In this section, in good, clear language you should describe the exact coverage of the problem. Thus, you tell your reader exactly what is and what is not a part of the problem.

4. Limitations. With some problems, you will find limitations which are of sufficient importance to warrant presenting them as a separate section of the introduction. By limitations, we mean anything which in some way has worked to impede the investigation or in some way has a deterring effect on the report. The illustrative list of limitations to a report investigation problem might include an inadequate supply of money for conducting the investigation, insufficient time for doing the work, unavoidable conditions which hampered objective investigation, or limitations existing within the problem under investigation.

5. Historical background. Sometimes a knowledge of the history of the problem is essential to a thorough understanding of the report. Thus, you may need to include in your introduction a section on the history of the problem. Your general aim in this part should be to acquaint your reader with some of the issues involved, some of the principles raised, and some of the values which might be received if more research were done. Also, in this section you may orient the reader and help to give him a better understanding of the report situation. This better understanding will theoretically help the reader and you, the writer, to solve some of the problems which may arise in the future.

6. Sources and methods of collecting data. It is usually advisable to tell the reader how you have collected the report information, whether through bibliographical research, through interviewing, and the like. If bibliographical research has been used, for example, you may give the library sources consulted and the major publications. If this latter list is long, you would be wise to append to the report a bibliography. Or, as another example, if your report has used interviewing, your description would cover such areas of the survey as sample determination, construction of the questionnaire, procedures followed in interviewing, facilities for checking returns, etc.

Whatever the technique used, you should describe it in sufficient detail to allow the reader to evaluate the quality of the work done.

7. Definitions. If your report is to make use of words likely to be unfamiliar to the reader, you should define these words somewhere in the report. One practice is to define each such word at the time of its first use in the report text. A more common practice, however, is to set aside a special section in the introduction for definitions.

8. Report preview. In long reports you should use a final section of the introduction to preview the report layout. In this section you should tell the reader how the report will be presented—what topics will be taken up first, second, third, etc. And of even greater importance, you should give the reasons why you follow this plan. Thus, you give your reader a clear picture of the road ahead, so that he may logically relate the topics of the report as he comes to them.

As previously noted, the sections discussed are listed only for the purpose of suggesting possible introduction content. In few reports will you need all of the topics mentioned. And in some instances you will be able to combine some of the topics; in other instances you may further split them into additional sections. In summary, you should tailor your introduction to fit the one report.

The report body. That part of the report which presents the information collected and relates it to the problem is the report body. Normally, it comprises the bulk of the content of a report. In fact, in a sense this part is the report. With the exception of the conclusion or recommendation section which follows, the other parts of the report are merely trappings. It is the report body to which most of our comments in this chapter and the following ones pertain.

The ending of the report. You may end your report in any of a number of ways: with a summary, a conclusion, a recommendation, or a combination of the three.

1. Summary. For some reports, particularly those which do little more than present fact, the end may consist of a summary of the major findings. Frequently, these reports follow the practice of having minor summaries at the end of each major division of the report. When you follow this practice, your final summary should simply recap these summaries. This form of summary, however, should not be confused with the synopsis. Like the summary, the synopsis presents a review of major findings; but unlike the summary, it contains the gist of the major supporting facts.

2. Conclusions. You draw your conclusions by inference (induction or deduction) from the facts and discussion in the body. Conclusions follow facts, even though in some reports they are placed at the beginning (the psychological arrangement).

Your conclusion should flow logically from the facts; but since this is a human process of interpretation, faulty conclusions may result. Consequently, conclusions are subject to opinions, be it rightly so or not.

For easy reference, you may tabulate your conclusions. But the arrangement of them is open to question. Sometimes you will feel that the most important ones should be placed first; sometimes you will want to list them according to the arrangements discussed in the findings. Also, you may combine them with recommendations. In some cases, where the conclusion is obvious, you may omit it and present only a recommendation.

3. Recommendations. The recommendations are the writer's section. Here you state your opinion based on the conclusions. Of course, you may not state your recommendations if you are not asked to; but if you are asked, you state them completely, including who should do what, when, where, why, and sometimes how.

You may include alternative courses of action. But you should state your preferences. Since you are familiar with the findings, you should not leave your reader on the horns of a dilemma. You should state his desired action and then leave him to choose his own course. Since you are likely to be in a staff position, you should give your advice for a line person to accept.

Appended parts

We did not mention two conventional report parts in our analysis of report structure. Primarily, we did not mention them because these parts play no role in the progression of report change. We use these parts whenever they are needed, irrespective of the report structure. One is the appendix.

Appendix. The appendix, as its name implies, is a section tacked on. It is used for supplementary information that supports the body of the report but has no logical place within the body of the report. Possible contents include questionnaires, working papers, summary tables, additional references, other reports, and so on.

As a rule, the charts, graphs, sketches, and tables that directly support the report should not be in the appendix. Instead, they should be in the body of the report where they support the findings.

Reports are best designed for the convenience of the reader. Obviously, it is not convenient for the reader to thumb through many pages in order to find an appendix illustration to the facts he reads in the report body.

Bibliography. The second of these parts is the bibliography. Investigations that make heavy use of secondary research normally require a list of the sources (such as books, periodicals, and newspapers) used. The bibliography is such a list. One acceptable arrangement for this list is discussed in Chapter 9.

Summary review of report construction

In summary, we have described generally a most formal report—one at the top step in our diagram (Figure 2-1). Now, by systematically omitting and/or changing some of the parts, you should be able to construct the type of report you need for a given situation.

Our description, of course, is oversimplified. Many companies prescribe report structures quite different from those described here. For example, some remove acknowledgments from the letter of transmittal or preface and place them in a separate prefatory section; some break up the synopsis and present conclusions, recommendations, and findings in separate prefatory sections; and some may include special prefatory sheets for intercompany routing purposes. Nevertheless, the progression we have described captures the relationship of all reports and should be helpful in planning yours.

THE MORE POPULAR SHORT REPORT FORMS

Although to this point we have given major emphasis to the long, formal report, the shorter, informal ones are by far the most common. Of the short report forms that you are likely to write, three in particular deserve our special attention. These are shown at the bottom of our illustration diagram of report structure (Figure 2-1) and are the short report, the letter report, and the memorandum report.

The short report

One of the more popular of the less imposing reports is the conventional short report (see illustration, Appendix B). Representing the fifth step in the diagram of report progression, this report consists of only a title page and the report text. Its popularity may be explained by the middle-ground impression of formality it gives. Inclusion of the one most essential of the prefatory parts gives the report at least a minimum appearance of formality. And it does this without the tedious work of preparing the other prefatory pages. It is ideally suited for the short but somewhat formal problem.

Like most of the less imposing forms of reports, the short report may be organized in either the direct or indirect order, although direct order is by far the most common plan. As illustrated by the report at the chapter end, this most common plan begins with a quick summary of the report, including and emphasizing conclusions and recommendations. Such a beginning serves much the same function as the synopsis of a long, formal report.

Following the summary are whatever introductory remarks are needed. As noted previously, sometimes this part is not needed at all. Usually, however, there follows a single paragraph covering the facts of authorization and a brief statement of the problem and its scope. After the introductory words come the findings of the investigation. Just as in the longer report forms, the findings are presented, analyzed, and applied to the problem. From all this comes a final conclusion and, if needed, a recommendation. These last two elements—conclusions and recommendations—may be presented at the end, even though they are also presented in the beginning summary. Sometimes, not to do so would end the report abruptly. It would stop the flow of reasoning before reaching its logical goal.

The mechanics of constructing the short report are much the same as those for the more formal, longer types. As illustrated in Chapter 8, this report uses the same form of title page and the same layout requirement. Like the longer reports, it makes use of captions. But because of the report's brevity, the captions rarely go beyond the two-division level. In fact, one level of division is most common. Like any other report, its use of graphic aids, appendix parts, and bibliography is dependent on its need for them.

Letter reports

As the wording implies, a letter report is a report written in letter form (see illustration, Appendix D). Primarily, it is used to present information to someone outside the company, especially when the report information is to be sent by mail. For example, a company's written evaluation of one of its credit customers may well be presented in letter form and mailed to the one who requests it. An outside consultant may write his analysis and recommendations in letter form. Or an organization officer may elect to report certain information to the membership in letter form.

Normally, letter reports are used to present the shorter problems—typically, those that can be presented in three or four pages or less. But no hard and fast rule exists on this point. Long letter reports (10 pages and more) have often been used successfully.

As a general rule, letter reports are written personally (using *I, you, we* references). Exceptions exist, of course, as when one is preparing such a report for an august group, such as a committee of the United States Senate or a company's board of directors. Other than this point, the writing style recommended for letter reports is much the same as that for any other report. Certainly, clear and meaningful expression is a requirement for all reports.

Letter reports may be arranged either in the direct or indirect order. If the report is to be mailed, there is some justification for using an indirect approach. As such reports arrive unannounced, an initial reminder of what they are, how they originated, and such is in order. A letter report written to the membership of an organization, for example, may appropriately begin with these words.

As authorized by your Board of Directors last January 6th, the following review of member company expenditures for direct-mail selling is presented.

If one elects to begin a letter report in the direct order, he would be wise to use a subject line. The subject line consists of some identifying words, which appear at the top of the letter, usually immediately after or before the salutation. Although they are formed in many ways, one acceptable version begins with the word "Subject" and follows it with descriptive words that identify the problem. As the following example illustrates, this identifying device helps to overcome any effect of confusion or bewilderment the direct beginning may otherwise have on the reader.

Subject: Report on direct-mail expenditures of
            Association members, authorized by Board of
            Directors January 1973

Association members are spending 8 percent more on direct-mail advertising this year than they did the year before. Current plans call for a 10 percent increase for next year.

Another possibility is to work the introductory identifying information into the direct opening material.

Regardless of which beginning is used, the organization plan for letter reports corresponds to those of the longer, more formal types. Thus, the indirect order letter report follows its introductory build-up with a logical presentation and analysis of the information gathered. From this presentation, it works logically to a conclusion and/or recommendation in the end. The direct order letter report follows the initial summary-conclusion-recommendation section with whatever introductory words are appropriate. For example, the direct beginning illustrated above could be followed with these introductory words.

> These are the primary findings of a study authorized by your Board of Directors last January. As they concern information vital to all of us in the Association, they are presented here for your confidential use.

Following such an introductory comment, the report would present the supporting facts and their analyses. The writer would systematically build up the case that supported his opening comment. With either order, when the report is sent as a letter it may close with whatever friendly goodwill comment is appropriate for the one occasion.

Memorandum reports

Memorandum reports are merely informal letter reports. They are used primarily for routine reporting within an organization, although some organizations use them for external communicating. Because they are internal communications, often they are informally written. In fact, they frequently are hurried, handwritten messages from one department or worker to another department or worker. The more formal memorandum reports, however, are well-written and carefully typed compositions (see Appendix C) that rival some more imposing types in appearance.

As far as the writing of the memorandum is concerned, all the instructions for writing letter reports apply. But memorandum reports tend to be more informal. And because they usually concern day-to-day problems, they have very little need for introductory information. In fact, they frequently may begin reporting without any introductory comment.

The memorandum report is presented on somewhat standardized interoffice memorandum stationery. The words *From, To,* and *Subject* appear at the page top (see Figure 8-10, page 159), usually following the company identification. Sometimes, the word *Date* also is included as a part of the heading. Like letters, the memorandum may carry a signature. In many offices, however, no typed signature is included, and the writer merely initials after his typed name in the heading.

SPECIAL REPORT FORMS

As noted previously, this review describes only generally the forms of the reports used in business. Countless variations exist. Of these variations, a few deserve special emphasis.

The staff report

One of the most widely used reports in business is the staff report. Patterned after a form traditional to the technical fields, the staff report is well adapted to business problem solving. Its arrangement follows the logical thought processes used in solving the conventional business problems. Although the makeup of this report varies by company, the following arrangement recommended by a major metals manufacturer is typical.

Identifying information: As the company's staff reports are written on intercompany communication stationery, the conventional identification information (To, From, Subject, Date) appears at the beginning.

Summary: For the busy executive who wants his facts fast, a summary begins the report. Some executives will read no further. Others will want to trace the report content in detail.

The problem (or objective): As in all good problem-solving procedures, the report text logically begins with a clear description of the problem—what it is, what it is not, what are its limitations, and such.

Facts: Next comes the information gathered in the attempt to solve the problem.

Discussion: Analyses of the facts and applications of the facts and analyses to the problem follow. (Frequently the statement of facts and the discussion of them can be combined.)

Conclusions: From the preceding discussion of facts comes the final meanings as they apply to the problem.

Recommendation: If the problem's objective allows for it, a course of action may be recommended on the basis of the conclusions.

Perhaps the major users of staff study reports are the branches of the Armed Forces. In all branches, this report is standardized. As shown in Figure 2-3, the military version differs somewhat from the business arrangement just described.

FIGURE 2-3
Military form of staff study report*

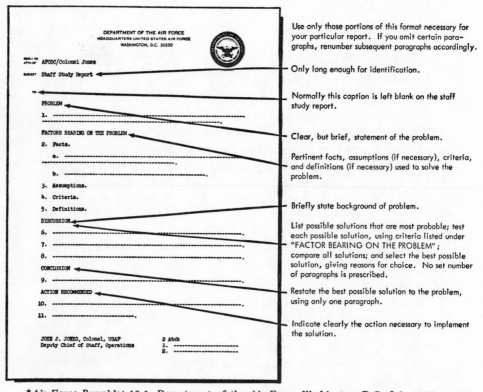

Air Force Pamphlet 10-1, Department of the Air Force, Washington, D.C., July 1969, p. 192.

The audit report

The short-form and long-form audit reports are well known to accountants. The short-form report is perhaps the most standardized of all reports—if, indeed, it can be classified as a report. Actually, it is a stereotyped statement verifying an accountant's inspection of a firm's financial records. The wording of the short-form audit report can be seen in the financial section of most corporate annual reports.

Composition of the long-form audit report is as varied as the short form is rigid. In fact, a national accounting association, after studying practices, concluded that no typical form exists. Although it covers a somewhat simple and limited audit, the audit report illustrated in Appendix E shows one acceptable form.

The technical report

Although often treated as a highly specialized form of report, the technical report differs primarily in its subject matter. Its form variations correspond to most of those discussed in this and the preceding chapter (see Appendix C). Even so, a somewhat conventional arrangement of the more formal research report has emerged.

This conventional arrangement begins much like the traditional formal report described earlier. First come the title pages, although frequently a routing or distribution form for intercompany use may be worked into them, or perhaps added to them. A letter of transmittal is likely to come next, followed by a table of contents and illustrations. From this point on, however, the technical report is likely to differ from the traditional one. These differences are mainly in the treatment of the information usually presented in the synopsis and the introduction of the conventional formal report.

Instead of the conventional synopsis, the technical report may present the summary information in various parts, such as findings, conclusions, and recommendations. Parts of the conventional introductory material also may be presented in prefatory sections. The objective is the most likely part in this area, although method is also a widely used section. The text usually begins with introductory information with remaining information organized as any conventional report. It may follow a predetermined and somewhat mechanical arrangement as: facts, discussion, conclusions, and recommendations.

3

Organizing the report

With the makeup of your report determined, you next turn to organizing your information for presentation. Let us now assume that you have all the information needed for your report. It is assembled before you in stacks of note cards, computer printouts, work sheets, and the like. Your task is to organize it into a communication that will tell those who need the information what they need to know.

PROBLEM ANALYSIS AND ITS CONTRIBUTION TO ORGANIZATION

Your information at this stage may be in various states of order. It can be a thoroughly disorganized mess of data or, more hopefully, an orderly and logically arranged set of information ready for report presentation. The state of order of your findings depends much on the plan you followed in your research. This research plan was probably the product of the preliminary analysis you made of your problem. More than likely, when you first thought through your problem, you began to structure it in your mind. You made decisions as to what information you would need and how the information would apply to your objective. And you made decisions which guided you in conducting your research, particularly about how to arrange the information as you gathered it.

Without question, the thinking you do on the problem before the research phase of your report is the beginning of your effort to organize your report. For this reason, even though we are skipping the research phase of the report work in this book, we shall review these thought processes.

Determination of the basic problem

Our review of these preliminary thought processes begins at the point when you first receive your report assignment. At this point, your initial effort should be to get your problem clearly in mind.

The preliminary investigation. Getting the problem in mind first requires that you gather all the information you need to understand it. Depending on the nature of your problem, this effort could take you through a variety of activities. It could require that you gather information from company files, talk over the problem with experts, search through bibliographical references, and/or discuss the problem with those authorizing the report. In general, you should investigate any source of information which will help you to understand your problem.

Clear statement of the problem. After you have sufficient information to understand the problem, your next logical step is to state it clearly. Preferably you should state it in writing. Stating the problem in writing is good for many reasons. A written statement is preserved permanently; thus, you may refer to it time and again without danger of changes occurring in it. In addition, other people can review, approve, and evaluate a written statement; and their assistance sometimes may be valuable. Most important of all, putting the problem in writing forces you to do, and to do well, the basic initial task of getting the problem in mind. In this way, this practice serves as a valuable form of self-discipline.

The problem statement normally takes one of three forms. One is the infinitive phrase: To determine the cause of decreasing sales at Store X. Another and equally good form is the question: What are the causes of decreasing sales at Store Y? A third and less popular form is the declarative statement. Although somewhat dull and not so solution-oriented as the other two, this form nevertheless gives a good indication of the problem. An example of it is the following: Company X sales are decreasing and it wants to know the cause for this decline.

Identification of the factors

From the problem statement you should next turn to the mental path of determining its needs. Within the framework of your logical imagination you should look for the factors of the problem. That is, you should look for the subject areas that must be investigated in order to satisfy the overall objective. Specifically, these factors may be of three types. First, they may be merely subtopics of the broader topics about which the report is concerned. Second, they may be hypotheses that must be subjected to the test of investigation and objective review. Third, in problems that involve comparisons they may be the bases on which the comparisons are made. Obviously, the process is a mental one, involving the intricate workings of the mind. Thus, we can describe it only in a most general way. You begin the process by applying your best logic and comprehensive abilities to the problem. The same mental process that helped you to comprehend your problem now should assist you in determining the structure of the solution.

Use of subtopics in information reports. If the problem concerns primarily a need for information, your mental effort should produce the main areas about which information is needed. Illustrating this type of situation is the problem of presenting for Company X a report that reviews the company's activities during the past quarter. Clearly, this is a routine and informational type of problem—that is, it requires no analysis, no conclusion, no recommendation. It requires only that information be presented. The mental process in this case is concerned simply with the determining of which subdivision of the overall subject should be covered. After thoroughly evaluating the possibilities, the investigator may come up with the following factor analysis.

Problem statement: To review operations of Company X from January 1 through March 31.
Factors:
1. Production.
2. Sales and promotion.
3. Financial status.
4. Plant and equipment.
5. Product development.
6. Personnel.

Hypotheses for problems of solution. Some problems by their nature seek a solution. Typically, such problems seek an explanation of a phenomenon or the correction of a condition. In analyzing such problems, you must seek possible explanations or solutions. Such explanations or solutions are termed *hypotheses*. After you determine the hypotheses, you test them and attempt to prove or disprove their applicability to the problem.

Illustrating problem analysis for this type of situation is the problem of a department store chain that seeks to learn why sales at one of its stores are dropping. In preparing this problem for investigation, the researcher logically would think of the possible explanations (hypotheses) of the decline in sales. He would be likely to think of more explanations than would be workable, so his task would be one of studying, weighing, and selecting. After such a study session, he may come up with explanations such as these.

Problem statement: Why have sales declined at the Milltown Store?
Factors:
1. Change in competition in the area.
2. Exceptional changes in area economy.
3. Merchandising deficiency.

Logically, in the investigation that follows the researcher would test each of the above hypotheses. Perhaps he would find that one, two, or all apply. Or perhaps he would find that none is logical. Then he would have to advance additional hypotheses for further evaluation.

Bases of comparison in evaluation studies. When your problem concerns evaluating something, either singularly or in comparison with others, your best plan is to determine the bases for the evaluation. More specifically, you should determine the characteristics that you will evaluate. In addition, sometimes you will need to determine the criteria to be used in evaluating each characteristic.

To illustrate this form of problem, take the assignment of determining whether air, electric, or hydraulic motors are best for a particular production task. Preliminary thinking in this stage might well lead to a problem statement like this:

Problem statement: To determine whether an air, electric, or hydraulic motor should be used to operate an angle valve.

Determining the factors would involve a search for the bases upon which this decision would rest. Certainly cost would be one. How each performs on the job would be another. Safety factors and maintenance problems relating to each motor could also be of some importance in the decision. Then there would be a variety of miscellaneous factors relating to the nature of each motor. Thus, the three motors might well be compared on these bases:

1. Cost.
2. Performance of task.
3. Maintenance.
4. Safety.
5. Miscellaneous factors.

Need for subbreakdowns

Each of the factors selected for investigation could have subbreakdowns (subfactors) of their own. In the problem comparing the three motors, for example, it would be necessary to look at a number of relative costs. There would be the initial cost, cost of operating, maintenance expense, and replacement cost, to name the most obvious. The broad factor of past performance also has subbreakdown possibilities. These might be control of torque and speed; problems of overload, reversals, and stalling; heat build-up; and smoothness in power flow. Other subfactor possibilities exist for the other factors. In fact, you might develop subbreakdowns for each of these subbreakdowns. You could continue this breakdown process as far as it would be helpful to you.

In summary, as you look at the information you have gathered for your problem, you are likely to find that it is somewhat organized. How much it is organized depends on the preliminary thinking you have given your problem and how you carried out this thinking in your research. More than likely, you have gathered and arranged your information by the problem's factors. If by chance you have collected your information without thinking through the problem, you would be wise to do so before proceeding further. Such mental effort is a logical first step in the organization process.

CONSTRUCTION OF THE REPORT OUTLINE

Now with your information collected and in preliminary workable order, you are ready to make an outline for your report. The outline, of course, is simply the plan you will use in the writing task which follows. It is to your report what the blueprint is to the construction engineer or what the pattern is to the dressmaker. In addition to guiding your work efforts, the outline compels you to think before you write. And when you think, your writing is likely to be clear.

Although the outline may be either written or mental, you will want to put it in written form for all except very short problems. In longer reports, where tables of contents are needed, the outline forms the basis of these tables. Also, in most long reports, and even in some short ones, the outline topics serve as guides to the reader as captions (headings) to the paragraphs of writing they cover.

Patterns of report organization

Before you begin the task of outlining, you will need to decide on which writing sequence, or pattern, to use in your report. Although many variations are found, two basic patterns exist. One is the indirect (also called logical and inductive); the other is the direct (also called psychological and deductive).

In the *indirect* arrangement, the findings appear in inductive order—moving from the known to the unknown. Preceding the report findings are whatever introductory material is necessary to orient the reader to the problem. Then come the facts, possibly with their analyses. And from these facts and analyses, concluding or summary statements are derived. In some problems, a recommendation section may also be included. Thus, in report form this arrangement is typified by an introductory section, the report body (usually made up of a number of sections), and a summary, conclusion, or recommendation section.

An illustration of this plan is the following report of a short and rather simple problem concerning a personnel action on a subordinate. For reasons of space economy, only the key parts of the report are presented.

> Numerous incidents during the past two months appear to justify an investigation of the work record of Clifford A. Knudson, draftsman, tool design department. . . .
>
> The investigation of his work record for the past two months reveals:
> 1. He has been late to work seven times.
> 2. He has been absent without acceptable excuse for seven days.
> 3. On two occasions he reported to work in a drunken and disorderly condition.
> 4. Etc.
>
> The foregoing evidence leads to one conclusion: Clifford A. Knudson should be fired.

Contrasting with the logical sequence is the *direct* arrangement. This sequence presents the subject matter in deductive fashion. Conclusions, summaries, or recommendations come first, and are followed by the facts and analyses they are drawn from. A typical report following such an order would begin with a presentation of summary, conclusion, and recommendation material. The report findings and the analyses from which the beginning section is derived comprise the following sections.

> Clifford A. Knudson, draftsman, tool design department, should be fired. This conclusion is reached after a thorough investigation brought about by numerous incidents during the past two months. . . .
> The recommended action is supported by this information from his work record for the past two months:
> 1. He has been late to work seven times.
> 2. He has been absent without acceptable excuse for seven days.
> 3. On two occasions he reported to work in a drunken and disorderly condition.
> 4. Etc.

As we observed in the preceding chapter, the direct sequence is used largely with shorter, day-to-day types of reports. It is used especially when conclusions are the main points of emphasis and the supporting facts and analyses are secondary. On the other hand, the indirect pattern is most useful in longer types of problems requiring a careful build-up, thorough analysis, and conclusion. But exceptions exist to this general observation, and you should use the one order that is best for your one case.

Obviously, as you choose the order for your report you will determine some of the structure of your outline. You will decide whether to use and where to place such parts as introduction, conclusion, summary, and recommendation. With these decisions behind you, your concern now is with arranging the findings and analyses (the body) of your report. It is primarily with this part that our discussion of outlining is concerned.

Systems of outline symbols

Another decision that you may need to make prior to beginning work on the outline is that concerning the system of symbols to use. As you know, outlining conventionally uses some system of symbols to designate the levels of the outline parts. Two such systems are commonly used, and you may choose either one.

The most commonly used system is the one you probably used throughout your school days. Commonly referred to as the conventional form, this system is best explained by illustration.

I. First degree of division.
  A. Second degree of division.
    1. Third degree of division.
      a. Fourth degree of division.
        (1) Fifth degree of division.
          (a) Sixth degree of division.

A second system of symbols is the numerical (sometimes called *decimal*) form. This system makes use of whole numbers to designate the major sections of a paper. Whole numbers followed by decimals and additional digits indicate subsections of the major sections. That is, an additional digit to the right of the decimal designates each successive step in the subdivision. Illustration best explains this procedure:

1. First degree of division.
  1.1 Second degree of division.
    1.11 Third degree of division.
      1.111 Fourth degree of division.
2. First degree of division.
  2.1 Second degree of division.
    2.11 Third degree of division (first item).
    2.12 Third degree of division (second item).
      2.121 Fourth degree of division (first item).
      2.122 Fourth degree of division (second item).

Care should be taken with numbers over 10. For example, 1.19 shows that this is item 9 of the third-degree of division, not the 19th item of the second degree, which would be written 1.(19).

Organization by division

Having selected the organization pattern and a symbol pattern for your report, you are ready to begin work on the outline itself. A logical place to begin this phase of your work is the problem statement developed at the beginning of your investigation. As we have noted, the problem statement tells you what your report must do.

Now you review the information you have collected to determine how it can be arranged to satisfy this objective. Largely, this effort is a mental one. You build the structure in your imagination. In the process, you hold large areas of facts and ideas in your mind, shifting them around until the most workable arrangement comes about.

Obviously, such mental efforts are impossible to describe, for minds work in different and complex ways. But we can review a general and systematic procedure for outlining that may prove helpful.

This procedure is based on the concept that outlining is a process of dividing. The subject of division is the whole of the information you have gathered. Thus, you begin by surveying this whole for some appropriate and logical means of dividing the information.

After you have divided the whole of your information into comparable parts, you may further divide each of the parts. Then, you may further divide each of these subparts, and you may continue to divide as far as it is practical to do so. Thus, in the end you may have an outline of two, three, or more levels (or stages) of division. You then designate these levels of division in your finished outline by the appropriate symbols from the system of symbols you have selected.

Division by conventional relationships

In dividing the information into subparts, you have the objective of finding a means of division that will produce equal and comparable parts. Time, place, quantity, and factor are the general bases for these divisions.

Whenever the information you have to present has some chronological aspect, organization by *time* is possible. In such an organization the divisions of the whole are periods of time. Usually, the periods follow a time sequence. Although a past-to-present or present-to-past sequence is the rule, variations are possible. The time periods you select need not be equal in length, but they should be comparable in importance. Determining comparability is, of course, a subjective process and is best based on the facts of the one situation.

A report on the progress of a research committee serves to illustrate this possibility. The time period covered by such a report might be broken down into the following comparable subperiods:

The period of orientation, May-July
Planning the project, August
Implementation of the research plan, September-November

The happenings within each period might next be arranged in the order of their occurrence. Close inspection might reveal additional division possibilities.

If the information you have collected has some relation to geographic location, you may use a *place* division. Ideally, the division would be such that like characteristics concerning the problem exist within each geographic area. Unfortunately, place divisions are hampered by the fact that political boundary lines and geographic differences in characteristics do not always coincide.

A report on the sales program of a national manufacturer illustrates a division by place. The information in this problem might be broken down by these major geographic areas:

New England
Atlantic Seaboard
South
Southwest
Midwest
Rocky Mountain
Pacific Coast

Another illustration of organization by place is a report on the productivity of a company with a number of manufacturing plants. A major division of the report might be devoted to each of the company's plants. The information for each of the plants might be further broken down by place, this time by sections, departments, divisions, or the like.

Quantity divisions are possible whenever your information has quantitative values. To illustrate, an analysis of the buying habits of a segment of the labor force could very well be broken down by income groups. Such a division might produce the following sections:

Under $2,000
$2,000 to under $4,000
$4,000 to under $7,000
$7,000 to under $10,000
$10,000 to under $15,000
Over $15,000

Another example of division on a quantitative basis is a report of a survey of men's preferences for shoes. Because of variations in preferences by ages, an organization by age groups might be used. Perhaps a division such as the following would be appropriate:

34

Youths, under 18
Young adult, 18-30
Adult, 31-50
Senior adult, 51-70
Elderly adult, over 70

Factor breakdowns are not so easily seen as the preceding three possibilities. Frequently, problems have little or no time, place, or quantity aspects. Instead, they require that certain information areas be investigated in order to meet the objectives. Such information areas may consist of a number of questions which must be answered in solving a problem. Or they may consist of subjects which must be investigated and applied to the problem.

An example of a division by factors is a report which seeks to determine the best of three cities for the location of a new manufacturing plant. In arriving at this decision, one would need to compare the three cities on the basis of the factors which affect the plant location. Thus, the following organization of this problem would be a logical possibility:

Worker availability
Transportation facilities
Public support and cooperation
Availability of raw materials
Taxation
Sources of power

Another illustration of organization by factors is a report advising a manufacturer whether to begin production of a new product. This problem has few time, place, or quantity considerations. The decision on the basic question will be reached by careful consideration of the factors involved. Among the more likely factors are these:

Production feasibility
Financial considerations
Strength of competition
Consumer demand
Marketing considerations

Combination and multiple division possibilities

Not all division possibilities are clearly time, place, quantity, or factor. In some instances, combinations of these bases of division are possible. In the case of a report on the progress of a sales organization, for example, the information collected could be arranged by a combination of quantity and place.

Areas of high sales activity
Areas of moderate sales activity
Areas of low sales activity

Although not so logical, the following combination of time and quantity is also a possibility:

Periods of low sales
Periods of moderate sales
Periods of high sales

The previously drawn illustration about determining the best of three towns for locating a new manufacturing plant shows that a problem may sometimes be divided by more than one characteristic. In this example the information also could have been organized by towns—that is, each town could have been discussed as a separate division of the report. This plan, however, is definitely inferior, for it separates physically the information which must be compared. Even so, it serves to illustrate a problem with multiple organization possibilities. The presence of two characteristics is common. The possibility of finding three or even four characteristics by which the information may be grouped is not remote. As a rule, when multiple division possibilities exist, those not used as a basis for the major division might serve to form the second and third levels of division. In other words, the outline to this problem might look like this:

II. Town A.
    A. Worker availability.
    B. Transportation facilities.
    C. Public support and cooperation.
    D. Availability of raw materials.
    E. Taxation.
    F. Sources of power.
III. Town B.
    A. Worker availability.
    B. Transportation facilities.
    C. Public support and cooperation.
    D. Availability of raw materials.
    E. Taxation.
    F. Sources of power.

IV. Town C.
   A. Worker availability.
   B. Etc.

Or it might look like this:

II. Worker availability.
   A. Town A.
   B. Town B.
   C. Town C.
III. Transportation facilities.
   A. Town A.
   B. Town B.
   C. Town C.
IV. Public support and cooperation.
   A. Town A.
   B. Town B.
   C. Town C.

The plan of organization selected should be the one which best presents the information gathered. Unfortunately, the superiority of one plan over the others will not always be so clear as in the illustration above. Only a careful analysis of the information and possibly trial and error will lead to the plan most desirable for any one problem.

Introductory and concluding sections

To this point, our discussion of organization procedures has concerned primarily the arrangement of information you have gathered and analyzed. It is the portion of the report that makes up what commonly is referred to as the report body. To this report body you may add additional sections. If, for example, you elected to follow the indirect order in your report, you would add an introduction at the beginning (the reason the examples above begin with II rather than I). To the end you would add a section to bring your report objective to a head. Perhaps you would need only a summary of your information for this final section. Or perhaps your findings and analyses would be drawn together to form a conclusion or recommendation. On the other hand, if you elected to use the direct order, you would lead off with your conclusion, recommendations, or summary facts, depending on what your report's goal happens to be. The introductory and body material would follow.

Wording the outline for report use

In the longer and more formal forms of reports, you will need to construct your outline in polished, written form, for you will use it in your report in two ways. First, it will serve as your table of contents, and second, as caption guides to the paragraphs of text. The following review of principles for wording outlines should help you in your efforts.

Topic or talking captions? In selecting the wording for the outline captions, you have a choice of two general forms—the topic and the talking caption. Topic captions are short constructions, frequently one or two words in length, which do nothing more than identify the topic of discussion. The following segment of a topic caption outline is typical of its type.

   II. Present armor unit.
       A.   Description and output.
       B.   Cost.
       C.   Deficiencies.
  III. Replacement effects.
       A.   Space.
       B.   Boiler setting.
       C.   Additional accessories.
       D.   Fuel.

Like the topic caption, the talking caption (or popular caption, as it is sometimes called) also identifies the subject matter covered. But it goes a step further. It also indicates what is said about the subject. In other words, the talking captions summarize, or tell the story of, the material they cover, as in the following illustration of a segment of a talking outline.

   II. Operation analyses of armor unit.
       A.   Recent lag in overall output.
       B.   Increase in cost of operation.
       C.   Inability to deliver necessary steam.
  III. Consideration of replacement effects.
       A.   Greater space requirements.

B. Need for higher boiler setting.
C. Efficiency possibilities of accessories.
D. Practicability of firing two fuels.

A Report Outline Made Up of Captions That Talk

I. Orientation to the problem.
    A. Authorization by board action.
    B. Problem of locating a woolen mill.
    C. Use of miscellaneous government data.
    D. Logical plan of solution.
II. Community attitudes toward the woolen industry.
    A. Favorable reaction of all cities to new mill.
    B. Mixed attitudes of all toward labor policy.
III. Labor supply and prevailing wage rates.
    A. Lead of San Marcos in unskilled labor.
    B. Concentration of skilled workers in San Marcos.
    C. Generally confused pattern of wage rates.
IV. Nearness to the raw wool supply.
    A. Location of Ballinger, Coleman, and San Marcos in the wool area.
    B. Relatively low production near Big Spring and Littlefield.
V. Availability of utilities.
    A. Inadequate water supply for all but San Marcos.
    B. Unlimited supply of natural gas for all towns.
    C. Electric rate advantage of San Marcos and Coleman.
    D. General adequacy of all for waste disposal.
VI. Adequacy of existing transportation systems.
    A. Surface transportation advantages of San Marcos and Ballinger.
    B. General equality of airway connections.
VII. A final weighting of the factors.
    A. Selection of San Marcos as first choice.
    B. Recommendation of Ballinger as second choice.
    C. Lack of advantages in Big Spring, Coleman, and Littlefield.

A Report Outline Made Up of Topic Captions

I. Introduction.
    A. Authorization.
    B. Purpose.
    C. Sources.
    D. Preview.

  II. Community attitudes.
      A. Plant location.
      B. Labor policy.
 III. Factors of labor.
      A. Unskilled workers.
      B. Skilled workers.
      C. Wage rates.
  IV. Raw wool supply.
      A. Adequate areas.
      B. Inadequate areas.
   V. Utilities.
      A. Water.
      B. Natural gas.
      C. Electricity.
      D. Waste disposal.
  VI. Transportation.
      A. Surface.
      B. Air.
 VII. Conclusions.
      A. First choice.
      B. Alternate choice.
      C. Other possibilities.

The choice between topic and talking captions usually is yours, although some companies have specific requirements for their reports. Topic captions are the conventional form. Because they have the support of convention, they are most often used in industry, especially in the more formal papers. Talking captions, on the other hand, are relatively new, but they are gaining rapidly in popularity. Either form is correct.

Parallelism of construction. Because of the many choices available, you are likely to construct an outline that has a mixture of grammatical forms. Some report writers believe that such a mixture of forms is acceptable and that each caption should be judged primarily by how well it describes the material it covers. The more precise and scholarly writers disagree, saying that mixing caption types is a violation of a fundamental concept of balance.

This concept of balance is expressed in a simple rule—the rule of parallel construction: All coordinate captions should be of the same grammatical construction. That is, if the caption for one of the major report parts (say, part II) is a noun phrase, all equal-level captions (parts III, IV, V) must be noun phrases. And if the first subdivision under a major section (say, Part A of II) is constructed as a sentence, the captions (B, C, D) coordinate with it must be sentences.

The following segment of an outline illustrates violation of the principles of parallel construction.

A. Machine output is lagging (sentence).
B. Increase in cost of operation (noun phrase).
C. Unable to deliver necessary steam (sentence fragment).

In this instance, you could make them parallel in any one of three ways. You could make the captions all sentences, all noun phrases, or all sentence fragments. If you want all noun phrases, for example, you could construct such captions as these.

A. Lag in machine output.
B. Increase in cost of operation.
C. Inability to deliver necessary steam.

If you want all sentences, you could write them like this.

A. Machine output is lagging.
B. Cost of operations increases.
C. Boiler cannot deliver necessary steam.

Another violation of parallelism is apparent in the following example.

A. Rising level of income (participial phrase).
B. Income distribution becoming uniform (sentence fragment).
C. Rapid advance in taxes (noun phrase).
D. Annual earnings rise steadily (sentence).

Again, you could correct them by selecting any one of the captions and revising the others to conform with it. As participial phrases, they may look like this.

A. Rising level of income.
B. Uniformly increasing income distribution.
C. Rapidly advancing taxes.
D. Steadily rising annual earnings.

You could revise them in noun phrases in this way.

A. Rise in level of income.
B. Uniform increase in income distribution.

C.   Rapid advance in taxes.
D.   Steady rise in annual earnings.

Or you could revise them as sentence fragments to read this way.

A.   Income level rising.
B.   Income distribution becoming uniform.
C.   Taxes advancing rapidly.
D.   Annual earnings rising steadily.

In constructing talking captions, you should work to make them the shortest possible word arrangement that also meets the talking requirement. Although the following captions talk well, their excessive lengths obviously affect their roles in communicating the report information.

Appearance is the most desirable feature that steady college users of cigarette lighters look for.

The two drawbacks of lighters mentioned most often by smokers who use matches are that lighters get out of order easily and frequently are out of fluid.

More dependability and the ability to hold more lighter fluid are the improvements most suggested by both users and nonusers of cigarette lighters.

Obviously, the captions contain too much information. Just what should be left out, however, is not easily determined. Much depends on the analysis the writer has given the material and what he has determined to be most significant. One analysis, for example, would support these revised captions.

Appearance most desirable feature.
Dependability primary criticism.
Fuel capacity most often suggested improvement.

Variety in expression. In the report outline, as in all forms of writing, you would be wise to use a variety of expressions. That is, you should take care not to overwork any words and expressions, for too-frequent repetitions tend to be monotonous. And monotonous writing is not pleasing to the discriminating reader. The following outline excerpts well illustrate this point.

A.   Chemical production in Texas.
B.   Chemical production in California.
C.   Chemical production in Louisiana.

As a rule, if you make the caption talk well, there is little chance of such monotonous repetition, for it is unlikely that successive sections would be presenting similar or identical information. That is, captions that are really descriptive of the material they cover are not likely to make use of the same words. As an illustration of this point, the outline topic in the foregoing example can be improved simply through making the captions talk.

A. Texas leads in chemical production.
B. California holds runner-up position.
C. Rapidly gaining Louisiana ranks third.

4

Qualities of
effective writing

The success of your report depends more on your writing skill than on any of your other efforts. Regardless of how well you organize your information or how appropriately you design your report makeup, it is your writing that counts most. Unless your report information is communicated effectively, you do not reach your goal, and your findings remain forever with you. Unfortunately, writing is not easy for most of us. In fact, it is likely to be the one report activity most people do worst.

How to improve your writing ability is no simple matter. The road to improvement is long, slow, and hard. There are no shortcuts, no easy-to-follow techniques—in fact, no guarantee of success. Even so, many practical procedures and techniques can be pointed out. And if you will learn and practice them, you cannot help but improve. The more practical and helpful of these procedures and practices appear in this and the following chapter.

FUNDAMENTAL NEED FOR ADAPTATION

Underlying all the following instructions on good report writing is the foundation principle of adaptation. By adaptation we mean fitting the message to the specific reader or readers of your writing.

Justification for this principle is obvious. It is a well-known fact that the communication abilities of writer and reader are not always equal. Probably no two people know precisely the same words; nor do they know equally much about all subject matter. Simply stated, if the writer uses words and concepts his reader does not know, he does not communicate. If the writer is to succeed, the words and concepts he uses must mean the same to him and to his reader.

Unfortunately, most of us do not adapt our writing to our reader without conscious effort. Chances are we find writing to be so much a chore that we accept whatever wording comes first to mind. Usually such wording communicates with someone just like us. But it misses its mark when the reader does not share our knowledge of words and subject matter.

Techniques for adapting

In adapting your writing to your reader, you should begin by visualizing him. You should get clearly in mind the answers to such questions as who he is, how much he knows about the subject, what his educational level is, and how he thinks. Then, with an image of your reader in mind, you should select the words which will communicate to him.

In many report situations, adapting to your reader will mean writing to a lower level than your own. Frequently, you will find yourself wishing to communicate with people below your educational level or with readers less knowledgeable than you are on the subject concerned. In both instances you will need to simplify your message. That is, you will need to write in the simple words and concepts your readers understand. If, for example, you are a company executive writing a memorandum to a group of factory employees, you would need to communicate in the everyday words of this group. Also when communicating on a technical subject to an educated but nontechnical reader, you would need to simplify the concepts in your message. Not to do so would be to miscommunicate, or at least to make communication difficult.

Your task in adapting is relatively simple when you are writing to a single reader or to a homogeneous group of readers. But what if you must write to a number of people with widely varying abilities? What should you do, for example, if your readers range from college graduates to those with almost no formal education? The answer is obvious. You would have no choice but to aim at the lowest level of the group. If you write at a higher level, you will be likely to miscommunicate with those at the lower level.

Cases of adaptation

Illustrating this fundamental principle are the following excerpts from the writings of the late Dr. Albert Einstein. When writing on a technical subject to a nontechnical audience, he skillfully adapted his words and concepts like this:

> What takes place can be illustrated with the help of our rich man. The atom M is a rich miser who, during his life, gives away no money (energy). But in his will he bequeaths his fortune to his sons M' and M'', on condition that they give to the community a small amount, less than one thousandth of the whole estate (energy or mass). The sons together have somewhat less than the father had (the mass sum M' and M'' is somewhat smaller than the mass M of the radioactive atom). But the part given to the community, though relatively small, is still so enormously large (considered as kinetic energy) that it brings with it a great threat of evil. Averting that threat has become the most urgent problem of our time.[1]

When writing to fellow scientists, however, Einstein wrote in the language they understood and expected.

> The general theory of relativity owes its existence in the first place to the empirical fact of the numerical equality of the inertial and gravitational mass of bodies, for which fundamental fact classical mechanics provided no interpretation. Such an interpretation is arrived at by an extension of the principle of relativity to co-ordinate systems accelerated relatively to one another. The introduction of co-ordinate systems accelerated relatively to inertial systems involves the appearance of gravitational fields relative to the latter. As a result of this, the general theory of relativity, which is based on the equality of inertia and weight, provides a theory of the gravitational field.[2]

Other good illustrations of adaptation appear in the annual reports of some of our major corporations. In attempting to communicate their financial information, some companies see their stockholders as being uninformed on matters of finance. Perhaps they see their rank-and-file readers as widows, housewives, and others who have not had business experience. Their communication might read like this:

> Last year your company's total sales were $117,400,000, which was slightly higher than the $109,800,000 total for the year before. After

---

[1] Albert Einstein, *Out of My Later Years,* Philosophical Library, Inc., New York, 1950, p. 53.
[2] Albert Einstein, *Essays in Science,* Philosophical Library, Inc., New York, 1934, p. 50.

deducting for all expenses, we had $4,593,000 left over for profits, compared with $2,830,000 for 1973. Because of these increased profits, we were able to increase your annual dividend payments per share from the 50 cents paid over the past ten years.

Some companies visualize their stockholders in an entirely different light and see them as being well informed in the language of finance. Perhaps they misjudge their readers, or maybe they fail to consider the readers' knowledge. In any event, these companies present their financial information in a somewhat technical and sophisticated manner, as illustrated by this example:

> The corporation's investments and advances in three unconsolidated subsidiaries (all in the development stage) and in 50 percent owned companies was $42,200,000 on December 31, 1973, and the excess of the investments in certain companies over net asset value at dates of acquisition was $1,760,000. The corporation's equity in the net assets as of December 31, 1973, was $41,800,000 and in the results of operations for the year ended December 31, 1973 and 1972, was $1,350,000 and $887,500. Dividend income was $750,000 and $388,000 for the years 1973 and 1972, respectively.

From the foregoing discussion and illustrations, some workable guidelines to adapting your writing appear. When you write to someone who is as well educated and informed on your subject as you are, your communication task is relatively easy. You need only to write to one like yourself, using language that is easy for you to understand. Likewise if you are a technical person writing on a technical subject to a technical reader who will understand the subject, you should write in the technical language both of you know and use. As technical language is the everyday language of the technician, this is the language which communicates quickly to him. Also, it is the language he expects. As we shall see later, however, such writing can be too technical even for the technical reader.

THE ESSENTIAL QUALITY OF READABILITY

Supporting the basic requirement of adaptation is the requirement that writing be readable. Readable writing is writing that communicates quickly—in a single reading. It communicates exactly—as precisely as language permits. And it communicates easily—with a minimum of effort for the reader. So important is this requirement, in fact, that it is the primary topic for discussion in Chapter 5. Although its techniques are better left for the next chapter, some general comments about readability are appropriate now.

In understanding this concept, it is important to keep in mind that readability is relative. That is, what is readable for one person may not be readable for another. As we noted in our discussion of adaptation, the explanation of this condition lies in the differences in the minds of people. Not all people understand the same words and concepts; nor are they equally able to comprehend the more complex sentence structures. From this observation we can conclude that levels of readability exist—that there is a level that is comprehensible for every reader.

It is important to note, also, that the existence of readability levels and the related principle of adaptation are not merely academic matters. They are realistic guides for writing soundly which are supported by exhaustive research over the past 30 years. In addition, this research has pointed out the two main causes of readability differences. They are sentence length and word difficulty. Thus, the shorter the sentences and the simpler the words, the lower is the level of readability. And the longer the sentences and more difficult the words, the higher is the level of readability. As we shall see, the specific techniques of writing reviewed in the next chapter are based on these findings.

Development of readability formulas

As a result of the readability research, a number of measures (or formulas) of readability have been developed. The purpose of these measures is to determine the level at which a given bit of writing is readable. Most such measures are based on sentence length and word difficulty—the two factors mentioned earlier which most influence readability.

Measuring sentence length is relatively easy, although a few complexities here and there do not meet the eye. Determining word difficulty, on the other hand, is somewhat complex. The studies show that word difficulty is traceable to many things—to historical origin, extent of usage, and such. But because normally the longer a word is the more difficult it is, word length is used in the formulas as a convenient gauge of word difficulty.

Of the various readability formulas used in business today, the

Gunning Fog Index probably is the most popular. Other formulas are just as accurate in measuring readability, but this one is among the easiest to use.

The Gunning Fog Index

The ease with which the Gunning Fog Index can be used is obvious from a review of the simple steps listed below. Its ease of interpretation is also obvious in that the index computed from these simple steps is in grade level of education. For example, an index of seven means that the material tested is easy reading for one at the seventh-grade level. An index of 12 indicates high school graduate level of readability. And an index of 16 indicates the level of the college graduate.

The simple steps for computing the index are as follows.

1. *Select a sample.* For long pieces of writing use at least 100 words. As in all sampling procedure, the larger the sample, the more reliable the results can be. So, in measuring readability for a long manuscript one would be wise to select a number of samples at random throughout the work.
2. *Determine the average number of words per sentence.* That is, first count words and sentences in a sample selected. Then divide the total number of words by the total of sentences.
3. *Determine the percentage of hard words in the sample.* Words of three syllables or longer are considered to be hard words. But do not count as hard words (1) words that are capitalized, (2) combinations of short, easy words *(grasshopper, businessman, book-keeper),* or (3) verb forms made into three-syllable words by adding *ed* or *es (repeated, caresses).*
4. *Add the two factors computed above and multiply by 0.4.* The product is the minimum grade level at which the writing is easily read.

Application of the Gunning Fog Index is illustrated with the following paragraph.

In *general, construction* of *pictograms* follows the *general procedure* used in *constructing* bar charts. But two special rules should be followed. First, all of the picture units used must be of equal size. The *comparisons* must be made wholly on the basis of the number of *illustrations* used and never by *varying* the *areas* of the *individual* pictures used. The reason for this rule is *obvious.* The human eye is grossly *inadequate* in *comparing areas* of *geometric* designs. Second, the pictures or symbols used must *appropriately* depict the *quantity* to be *illustrated.* A *comparison* of the navies of the world, for *example,* might make use of *miniature* ship drawings. Cotton *production* might be shown by bales of cotton. *Obviously,* the drawings used must be *immediately interpreted* by the reader.

Inspection of the paragraph reveals these facts. It has 10 sentences and 129 words for an average sentence length of 13. Of the total of 129 words, 26 are considered to be hard words. Thus, the percentage of hard words is 20. From these data, the Gunning Fog Index is computed as follows.

```
Average sentence length . . . . . . . . . . . .   13
Percentage of hard words  . . . . . . . . . .   20
Total . . . . . . . . . . . . . . . . . . . . . .   33
Multiply by . . . . . . . . . . . . . . . . . . .  0.4
Grade level of readership . . . . . . . . . . . 13.2
```

Critical appraisal of the formulas

Readability formulas are widely used in business today. Perhaps the reason for their popularity is the glitter of their apparent mathematical exactness. Or perhaps they are popular because they reduce to simple and workable formulas the most complex work of writing. Whatever the reason, you will be wise to look at the formulas objectively.

Unquestionably, these formulas have been a boon to improving clarity in report writing. They emphasize the main causes of failure in written communication. And they provide a convenient check and measure of the level of one's writing. But they also have some limitations.

The most serious limitation of the formulas is the primer style of writing that can result if you use them slavishly. If you are not careful, they can lead you to overuse simple words and to write a monotonous succession of short sentences. The result is dull reading. Dull reading does not hold your reader's attention. And without your reader's attention, you are not likely to communicate with him.

Perhaps the formulas will be most useful to you if you are an unskilled writer. By intelligent use of the formulas, you may at least improve the communication quality of your work. Your writing style, which was not so good to begin with, does not suffer. If you are a skilled writer, on the other hand, you can violate the formulas and still communicate. Charles Dickens, for example, was a master at communicating in clear yet long sentences. So was Alexander Pope. And so are many report writers. If you fall somewhere between these extremes in writing ability, the wisest course for you is to use the formulas as general guides. But you should keep in mind that a formula will never replace the clear and logical thinking that is the underpinning of all clear writing.

THE IMPORTANCE OF OBJECTIVITY

Objectivity, a basic quality of good report writing, concerns both your attitude as the writer and writing style. You as the writer should strive to maintain an objective attitude by divorcing your prejudices and emotions from your work and by fairly reviewing and interpreting the information you have uncovered. Thus, you should approach your problem with an open mind and look at all sides of each question. Your role should be much like that of a judge presiding over a court of law. You are not moved by personal feelings. You seek the truth, and you leave no stones unturned in the quest for it. You make your decision only after carefully weighing all of the evidence uncovered.

Objectivity as a basis for believability

A report built on the quality of objectivity has another ingredient essential to good report writing. That ingredient is believability. Perhaps biased writing can be in language that is artfully deceptive and may at first glance be believable. But such writing is risky. If at any spot in the report the reader detects bias, he will be suspicious of the whole work. Painstaking objectivity, therefore, is the only sure way to believable report writing.

Objectivity and the question of impersonal versus personal writing

Recognizing the need for objectivity, the early report writers worked to develop a writing style that would convey this attitude. They reasoned that the source of the subjective quality in a report is the human being. And they reasoned that objectivity is best attained by emphasizing the factual material of a report rather than the personalities involved. So they worked to remove the human being from their writing. Impersonal writing style was the result. By impersonal writing is meant writing in the third person—without I's, we's, or you's.

In recent years, impersonal writing has been strenuously questioned by many writers. These writers point out that personal writing is more forceful and direct than is impersonal writing. They contend that writing that brings both reader and writer into the picture is more like conversation and therefore more interesting. And in regard to objectivity they answer that objectivity is an attitude of mind and not a matter of person. A report, they say, can be just as objective when written in personal style as when written in impersonal style. Frequently, they counter with the argument that impersonal writing leads to an overuse of passive voice and a generally dull writing style. This last argument, however, lacks substance. Impersonal writing can and should be interesting. Any dullness it may have is wholly the fault of the writer. As proof one has only to look at the lively styles used by the writers for newspapers, news magazines, and journals. Most of this writing is impersonal—and usually it is not dull.

As in most cases of controversy, there is some merit to the arguments on both sides. There are situations in which personal writing is best. There are situations in which impersonal writing is best. And there are situations in which either style is appropriate. The choice is yours. You must decide at the outset of your work which style is best for the one situation.

Your decision should be based on the unique circumstances of your report situation. First, you should consider the expectations or desires of those who will read the report. Often, you will find a preference for the impersonal style, for, like most human beings, your readers are likely to be reluctant to break tradition. Next, you should consider the formality of the situation. If your situation is informal, as when the report is really a personal communication of information between associates, personal writing is appropriate. But if your situation is formal, as is so with most major reports, the conventional impersonal style is best.

Perhaps the distinction between impersonal and personal writing is best made by illustration.

Personal	*Impersonal*
Having studied the various advantages and disadvantages of using trading stamps, I conclude that your company should not adopt this practice. If you use the stamps, you would have to pay out money for them. Also, you would have to hire additional employees to take care of the increase in sales volume.	A study of the advantages and disadvantages of using trading stamps supports the conclusion that the Mills Company should not adopt this practice. The stamps themselves would cost extra money. Also, use of stamps would require additional personnel to take care of the increase in sales volume.

CONSISTENCY IN TIME VIEWPOINT

A major problem in keeping order in a report is that of fitting all of the details in their proper place in time. Not to do so would be to confuse the reader and to bring up unnecessary barriers in the communication effort. Thus, it is important that in your report you maintain a proper time viewpoint.

Maintaining a proper time viewpoint in the report is a problem for even the seasoned writer. Illogical shifts from one tense to another detract generally from the writing and mar the accuracy of the presentation. Consistency in time viewpoint is the one logical solution to the problem. But whether the consistent time viewpoint should be past or present is a matter on which opinions differ.

Some authorities favor a consistent past viewpoint. They assume that all the data collected, as well as the research and the writing of the report, are past events by the time the report is read. Thus, they conclude that it is logical to report a result from the current survey in words such as "22 percent of the managers *favored* a change." And they would write a reference to another part of the report in words like these: "In Chapter 2, this conclusion *was* reached."

A more logical approach is to write in the present-time viewpoint. In following this viewpoint, you would present as current all information which is current at the time of writing. For example, a presentation of the results of a recent survey might be made in words like these: "Twenty-two percent of the managers *favor* a change." Or a reference in the report to another part of the report might be in words like "In Chapter 2, this conclusion *is* reached." Information which is clearly in the past or in the future at the time of writing, however, you should present in a past or future tense. For example, survey findings likely to be obsolete at the time of writing might be worded thus: "In 1939, 44.2 percent of the managers *favored* this plan." Or a predicted figure for the future might be reported in these words: "According to this projection, the value of these assets will exceed $32 million by 1980." A present-time viewpoint should in no way be interpreted to mean that every verb must be in the present tense. Nor should it ever result in placing a single event awkwardly in time. Adherence to this viewpoint simply involves placing all facts in their logical place in time at the time of writing.

STRUCTURAL AIDS TO REPORT COHERENCE

Smooth flow of thought and clear relationships between the facts presented are essential to successful communication of the report information. Unless the relationships of the details are made clear, unless the reader is made to see the logic of your presentation, he is not likely to receive the full communication effect of your report message. The writing technique which gives your report this desired effect is coherence.

Probably the one most important thing you can do to make your report coherent is to organize it logically—a topic discussed earlier. If you relate facts in a logical, natural sequence, your writing will have some degree of coherence. For the shorter reports, good organization provides the bulk of the coherence you need for clear communication. But for most longer works, particularly long, involved analytical reports, you will need to do more. In such reports the relationships of the parts tend to be complex, and readers do not grasp them so easily. Thus, when you write such reports you will need to make a special effort to structure the punctuation so that all relationships of contents are clear. Specifically, you can structure the report story by using concluding and summary paragraphs to mark the report progress. You can use introductory and preview paragraphs to show major relationships. And you can use transitional sentences and words to show relationships between the lesser parts.

The use of introductory, concluding, and summarizing sections

The extent of use of introductory, concluding, and summarizing sections depends on the report. Perhaps the best rule for you to follow is to use them whenever they are needed to relate the parts of the report or to move the report message along. In general, these

sections are more likely to be needed in the longer and more involved reports. In such a report you are likely to follow a traditional
plan of connecting structure.

This plan, as described in Figure 4-1, uses these special sections to
tie together all the parts of the report. Because it serves to keep the
reader aware of where he has been, where he is, and where he is
going, the plan helps him to find his way through a complex problem. Also, placement of forward-looking and backward-glancing
sections permits the casual reader to dip into the report at any place
and quickly get his bearing.

As noted in Figure 4-1, you may use three types of sections
(usually a paragraph or more) to structure the report. One is the
introductory preview. Another is the section introduction. And still
another is the conclusion or summary sections, either for the major
report parts or for the whole report.

For a longer report you may use a section of the report introduction (see Chapter 3) to tell the reader of the report's organization
plan. Generally, this preview covers three things: topics to be discussed, their order of presentation, and the logic for this order.

FIGURE 4-1

Diagram of the structural coherence plan of a long formal report

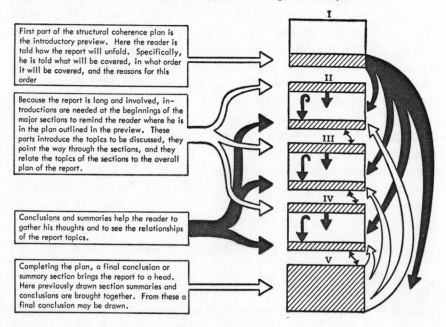

Having been informed of the basic plan, the reader is then able to understand quickly how each new subject he encounters in the following pages fits into the whole. Thus, a connection between the major report parts is made. The following paragraphs do a good job of previewing a report comparing four brands of automobiles for use by a sales organization:

The decision as to which light car Allied Distributors should buy is reached through a comparison on the basis of three factors: cost, safety, and dependability. Each of these major factors is broken down into its component parts, which are applied to each make being considered.

Because it is the most tangible factor, cost is examined first. In this section the four makes are compared for initial and trade-in values. Then they are compared for operating costs as determined by gasoline mileage, oil usage, repair expense, and the like. In a second major section the same comparison is used to determine car safety. Driver visibility, special safety features, brakes, steering quality, acceleration rate, and traction are the main considerations here. In a third section, dependability of the cars is measured on the basis of repair records and salesmen's time lost because of automobile failure. In a final section, weights are assigned to the foregoing comparisons, and the brand of automobile best suited for the company's needs is recommended.

In addition to the introductory preview, you may help show relationships between the major report topics by introductory and summary sections placed at convenient spots throughout the report. You may use sections occasionally to remind the reader of where he is in the progress of the report. Also, you may use them to elaborate on the relationships between the report parts and, in general, to give detailed connecting and introductory information. The following paragraph, for example, serves as an introduction to the final section of a report of an industrial survey. Note how the paragraph ties in with the preceding section, which covered industrial activity in three major geographic areas, and justifies covering secondary areas.

Although the great bulk of industry is concentrated in three areas (Grand City, Milltown, and Port Starr), a thorough industrial survey needs to consider the secondary, but nevertheless important, areas of the state. In the rank of their current industrial potential, these areas are the Southeast, with Hartsburg as its center; the Central West, dominated by Parrington; and the North Central, where Pineview is the center of activities.

The following summary-conclusion paragraph gives an appropriate ending to a major section. The paragraph brings to a head the find-

ings presented in the section and points the way to the subject of
the next section.

These findings and those pointed out in preceding paragraphs all lead
to one obvious conclusion. The small-business executive is concerned
primarily with subject matter which will aid him directly in his work.
That is, he favors a curriculum slanted in favor of the practical subjects.
He does, however, insist on some coverage of the liberal areas. Too, he is
convinced of the value of studying business administration. On all of
these points he is clearly out of tune with the bulk of big-business leaders
who have voiced their positions in this matter. Even the most dedicated
business administration professors would find it difficult to support such
an extremely practical concept. Nevertheless, these are the small-business
executive's opinions on the subject; and as he is the consumer of the
business education product, his opinion should at least be considered.
Likewise, his specific recommendation on courses (subject of the following
chapter) deserves careful review.

Proper use of paragraphs such as these forms a network of connection throughout the work. The longer the report, the more effective
they are likely to be.

Communication value of transition

Transition, which literally means "a bridging-across," may be
formed in many ways. In general, transitions are made by words, or
sentences, placed in the writing to show the relationships of the
information presented. They may appear at the beginning of discussion on a new topic and may relate this topic to what has been
discussed. They may appear at the end as a forward look. Or they
may appear internally as words or phrases which in various ways tend
to facilitate the flow of subject matter.

Whether you should use a transition word or sentence in a particular place depends on the need for relating the parts concerned.
Because the relationship of its parts may be seen merely from a
logical sequence of presentation, a short report might require only
a few transitional parts here and there. A long and involved report,
on the other hand, might require much more transitional help.

A word of caution. Before more specific comments on transition
are given, one fundamental point must be made clear. You should
not make transitions mechanically. You should use them only when
there is need for them, or when leaving them out would produce
abruptness in the flow of report findings. You should not make them

abruptness in the flow of report findings. You should not make them appear to be stuck in; instead, you should make them blend in naturally with the surrounding writing. For example, you should avoid transitional forms of this mechanical type: "The last section has discussed topic X. In the next section topic Y will be analyzed."

Transitional sentences. Throughout the report, you can improve the connecting network by the judicious use of sentences. You can use them especially to form the connecting link between secondary sections of the report, as illustrated in the following example of transition between sections B and C of a report. The first few lines of this illustration draw a conclusion for section B. Then, with smooth tie-in, the next words introduce section C and relate this topic to the report plan.

> [Section B, concluded]
> . . . Thus the data show only negligible difference in the cost for oil consumption [subject of section B] for the three brands of cars.
> [Section C]
> Even though costs of gasoline [subject of section A] and oil [subject of section B] are the more consistent factors of operation expense, the picture is not complete until the cost of repairs and maintenance [subject of section C] is considered.

Additional examples of sentences designed to connect succeeding parts are the following. By making a forward-looking reference, these sentences set up the following subject matter. Thus, the resulting shifts of subject matter are both smooth and logical.

> These data show clearly that Edmond's machines are the most economical. Unquestionably, their operation by low-cost gas and their record for low-cost maintenance give them a decided edge over competing brands. *Before a definite conclusion as to their merit is reached, however, one more vital comparison should be made.*

(The final sentence clearly introduces the following discussion of an additional comparison.)

> . . . *At first glance the data appear to be convincing, but a closer observation reveals a number of discrepancies.*

(Discussion of the discrepancies is logically set up by this final sentence.)

Placement of topic sentences at key points of emphasis is still another way of using a sentence to improve the connecting network of the report. Usually, the topic sentence is best placed at the paragraph beginning where the subject matter can very quickly be related to its spot in the organization plan described in the introductory preview or the introduction to the section. Note, in the following example, how the topic sentences emphasize the key information. Note also how the topic sentences tie the paragraphs with the preview (not illustrated), which no doubt related this organization plan.

Brand C accelerates faster than the other two brands, both on level road and on a 9 percent grade. According to a test conducted by Consumption Research, brand C attains a speed of 60 miles per hour in 13.2 seconds. To reach this same speed, brand A requires 13.6 seconds, and brand B requires 14.4 seconds. On a 9 percent grade, brand C reaches the 60-mile-per-hour speed in 29.4 seconds and brand A in 43.3 seconds. Brand B is unable to reach this speed.

Because it carries more weight on its rear wheels than the others, brand C has the best traction of the three. Traction, which means a minimum of sliding on wet or icy roads, is most important to safe driving, particularly during the cold, wet winter months. As traction is directly related to the weight carried by the rear wheels, a comparison of these weights should give some measure of the safety of the three cars. According to data released by the Automobile Bureau of Standards, brand C carries 47 percent of its weight on its rear wheels. Brands B and A carry 44 and 42 percent, respectively.

Transitional words. Although the major transition problems concern connection between sections of the report, there is need also for transition between lesser parts. If the writing is to flow smoothly, you will need to relate clause to clause and sentence to sentence and paragraph to paragraph. Transitional words and phrases generally serve to make these connections.

The transitional words you may use are too numerous to relate, but the following review is a clear picture of what these words are and how they can be used. With a little imagination to supply the context, you can easily see how such words relate succeeding ideas. For better understanding, the words are grouped by the relationships they show between subjects previously discussed and those to be discussed.

Relationship	*Word examples*
Listing or enumeration of subjects	In addition
	First, second, etc.
	Besides
	Moreover

Relationship	*Word examples*
Contrast	On the contrary
	In spite of
	On the other hand
	In contrast
	However
Likeness	In a like manner
	Likewise
	Similarly
Cause-result	Thus
	Because of
	Therefore
	Consequently
	For this reason
Explanation or elaboration	For example
	To illustrate
	For instance
	Also
	Too

THE ROLE OF INTEREST IN REPORT COMMUNICATION

Like all forms of good writing, report writing should be interesting. Actually, the quality of interest is as important as the facts of the report, for without interest, communication is not likely to occur. If his interest is not held—if his mind is allowed to stray—the reader cannot help missing parts of the message. And it does not matter how much the reader wants to read the report message; nor is his interest in the subject enough to assure communication. The writing must maintain this interest. The truth of this reasoning is evident to you if you have ever tried to read dull writing in studying for an examination. How desperately you wanted to learn the subject, but how often your mind strayed away!

Perhaps writing interestingly is an art. But if it is, it is an art in which you can gain some proficiency if you work at it. If you are to develop this proficiency, you need to work watchfully to make your words build concrete pictures, and you need to avoid the "rubber-stamp" jargon or technical talk so often used in business. You must cultivate a feeling for the rhythmic flow of words and sentences. You must remember that back of every fact and figure there is some form of life—people doing things, machines operating, a commodity being marketed. The secret of quality writing is to bring the real life to the surface by concrete diction and vigorous active-voice verbs insofar as it is possible. But at the same time, you should work to achieve interest without using more words than are necessary.

Here a word of caution may be injected. Attempts to make writing style interesting can be overdone. Such is the case whenever the reader's attention is focused on how something is said rather than on what is said. Good style, to be effective, simply presents information in a clear, concise, and interesting manner. Possibly the purpose and definition of style can best be summarized by this objective of the report writer: Writing style is at its best when the readers are prompted to say "Here are some interesting facts" rather than "Here is some beautiful writing."

DIFFERENCES IN SHORT AND LONG REPORTS

The report-writing instruction we have reviewed thus far applies generally to all reports. But as you no doubt have observed through personal experience, the shorter forms of reports tend to differ somewhat from the longer ones. These differences do not concern much of the writing instruction we have reviewed. All report writing should be readable. Objectivity is a universal requirement. And consistency in time viewpoint is as important to the longest report as it is to the shortest. But important differences exist—four in particular. In general, the shorter reports (1) have less need for introductory material, (2) are more likely to be written in the direct order, (3) tend to use a more personal writing style, and (4) have less need for a formal coherence plan. Although only two of the four concern writing qualities, for convenience we shall discuss all of them here.

Less need for introductory material

One major content difference in the shorter report forms is their minor need for introductory material. Most reports at this level concern day-to-day problems. Thus, these reports have a short life. They are not likely to be kept on file for posterity to read. They are intended for only a few readers, and these few know the problem and its background. The reader's interests are in the findings of the report and any action it will lead to.

This is not to say that all shorter forms have no need for introductory material. In fact, some have very specific needs. In general, however, the introductory need in the shorter and more informal reports is less than that for the more formal and longer types. But no rule can be applied across the board. Each case should be analyzed individually. In each case, you must cover whatever introductory material is needed to prepare your reader to receive the report. In some shorter reports, an incidental reference to the problem, authorization of the investigation, or such will do the job. In some extreme cases, you may need a detailed introduction comparable to that of the more formal report. There are reports, also, that need no introduction whatever. In such cases, the nature of the report serves as sufficient introductory information. A personnel action, for example, by its very nature explains its purpose. So do weekly sales reports, inventory reports, and some progress reports.

Predominance of direct order

Because usually they are more goal-oriented, the shorter more informal reports are likely to use the direct order of presentation. That is, typically such reports are written to handle a problem—to make a specific conclusion or recommendation of action. This conclusion or recommendation is of such relative significance that it by far overshadows the analysis and information that support it. Thus, it deserves a lead-off position.

As noted earlier, the longer forms of reports may also use a direct order. In fact, many of them do. The point is, however, that most do not. Most follow the traditional logical (introduction, body, conclusion) order. As one moves down the structural ladder toward the more informal and shorter reports, however, the need for direct order increases. At the bottom of the ladder, direct order is more the rule than the exception.

Your decision of whether or not to use the direct order is best based on a consideration of your reader's likely use of the report. If the reader needs the report conclusion or recommendation as a basis for an action he must take, directness will speed his effort. A direct presentation will permit him to quickly receive the most important information. If he has confidence in your work, he may not choose to read beyond this point, and he can quickly take the action the report supports. Should he desire to question any part of the report, however, it is there for his inspection. The obvious result would be to save the valuable time of a busy executive.

On the other hand, if there is reason to believe that your reader will want to arrive at the conclusion or recommendation only after a logical review of the analysis, you should organize your report in the indirect (logical) order. Especially would this arrangement be preferred when your reader does not have reason to place his full confidence in your work. If you are a novice working in a new assignment, for example, you would be wise to lead your reader to your recommendation or conclusion by using the logical order.

More personal writing style

Although the writing that goes into all reports has much in common, that in the shorter reports tends to be more personal. That is, the shorter reports are likely to use the personal pronouns *I, we, you,* and such rather than a strict third-person approach.

The explanation of this tendency toward personal writing in short reports should be obvious. In the first place, the situation that gives rise to a short report usually involves more personal relationships. Such reports tend to be from and to people who know each other— people who normally address each other informally when they meet and talk. In addition, the shorter reports by their nature are apt to involve a personal investigation. The finished work represents the personal observations, evaluations, and analyses of the writer. He is expected to report them as his own. A third explanation is that the shorter problems tend to be the day-to-day routine ones. They are by their very nature informal. It is logical to report them informally, and personal writing tends to produce this informal effect.

As explained earlier, your decision on whether to write a report in personal or impersonal style should be based on the circumstances of the situation. You should consider the expectations of those who will receive the report. If they expect formality, you should write impersonally. If they expect informality, you should write personally. Second, if you do not know the reader's preferences, you should consider the formality of the situation. Convention favors impersonal writing for the most formal situation.

From this analysis, it should be apparent that either style can be appropriate for reports ranging from the shortest to the longest type. The point is, however, that short report situations are most likely to justify personal writing.

Less need for coherence plan

As is pointed out previously, the longer forms of reports need some form of coherence plan to make the parts stick together. That is, because of the complexities brought about by length, the writer must make an effort to relate the parts. Otherwise, the paper would read like a series of disjointed minor reports. What he does is to use summaries and introductory forward-looking sentences and paragraphs at key places. Thus, the reader is able to see how each part of the report fits into the whole scheme of things.

The shorter the report becomes, the less is its need for such a coherence plan. In fact, in the extremely short forms (such as memorandum and letter reports), little in the way of wording is needed to relate the parts. In such cases, the information is so brief and simple that a logical and orderly presentation clearly shows the plan of presentation.

Although coherence plans are less frequently used in the short forms of reports, the question of whether to include them should not be arbitrarily determined by length alone. Instead, the matter of need should guide you in your choice. Whenever your presentation contains organization complexities that can be made clear by summaries, introductions, and relating parts, these coherence elements should be included. Thus, need rather than length is the major determinant. But it is clearly evident that need for coherence decreases as the report length decreases.

5

Techniques of
readable writing

Your ultimate goal as a report writer is to communicate the report message. Ideally, you should communicate your message as quickly, as easily, and as precisely as language will permit. As explained in Chapter 4, quick, easy, and precise communication is built on certain basic writing characteristics that you should understand thoroughly. Specifically, you should understand that good report writing is adapted to the reader's level. Good report writing is also readable. And in this regard, you should know how to use readability study conclusions that word difficulty and sentence length are major determinants of readability. Your writing should be interesting if it is to communicate—dull writing can lull the reader and thereby defeat the communication effort.

Knowledge of all these characteristics, however, gives only a general appreciation of good report writing. The application of this general knowledge to the task of report writing requires specific knowledge of techniques. Some of the more useful techniques are presented in the following pages. They are grouped by the three basic units of writing—the word, the sentence, and the paragraph.

Before taking up these specific techniques, however, one qualifying point should be stressed. These techniques are not to be applied mechanically. Instead, they must be tempered with reason. Writing is not routine work to be done by the numbers, by rules, or by formulas. Rather it is to some extent an art. As in all forms of art, mastery of techniques is a prerequisite to good performance. In writing, perhaps more than in any other art, the techniques must be applied with good judgment.

WORD SELECTION

In general, your task in writing is to produce in your reader's mind the meanings formulated in your mind. To do this, you use written symbols of meaning (words). Your task is largely one of selecting words that exactly relate the intended meanings.

The very nature of words, however, makes this task difficult. A glance at the size of an unabridged dictionary dramatically explains this difficulty. In addition to the great number of words in the language, your difficulty is intensified by the complexity of word meaning. Words are at best inexact symbols of meaning. A single word may have a dozen dictionary meanings. In fact, it is said that the 500 most commonly used English words have a total of 14,000 dictionary definitions—an average of 28 meanings per word. No doubt in each of our minds additional shades of difference in meaning exist. Contributing further to this difficulty is the inexactness with which most of us use words.

The complex nature of words makes your task more difficult. Perhaps this difficulty is too much involved for even the best writers to overcome completely. But certainly any writer can improve his communication ability by understanding these limitations and by making deliberate effort to overcome them.

Selecting words the reader understands

A major requirement of writing that communicates is that the words used mean the same to both the writer and the reader. In many instances in business, this requirement means simplifying the writing. Certainly, you can justify simplification when you write to people of a lower intellectual level. Even in writing to intellectual equals, you may find need to simplify.

This suggestion, however, should in no way be interpreted as an unqualified endorsement of primer writing. When you write for technical or other learned people on subjects about which they are well informed, you should write in words they expect and understand. But even in such cases, you will find some degree of simplification to be a key to quick and correct communication. As we noted in Chapter 4, the readability studies support simplified writing. They show conclusively that writing communicates best when it is slightly below the comprehension level of the reader. Specifically, they show that simplification is achieved through a general preference for the familiar over the unfamiliar, for the short over the long, and for the nontechnical over the technical word. Although these distinctions between words overlap considerably, we shall discuss them separately for reasons of emphasis.

Use the familiar words. The first rule of word selection is to use the familiar everyday words. Of course, the definition of familiar words varies by persons. What is everyday usage to some people is likely to appear to be high-level talk to others. Thus, the suggestion to use familiar language is in a sense a specific suggestion to apply the principle of adapting the writing to the reader.

Unfortunately, many business writers do not use everyday language enough. Instead, they tend to change character when they begin to put their thoughts on paper. Rather than writing naturally, they become stiff and stilted in their expression. For example, instead of using an everyday word like *try*, they use the more unfamiliar word *endeavor* They do not "find out"; they "ascertain." They "terminate" rather than "end," and they "utilize" instead of "use."

How such thinking can cloud meaning in a report is well illustrated by a happening in the space program at Cape Canaveral. According to a news release, scientists at Cape Canaveral had been experimenting with monkeys in preparation for prolonged space travel. The monkeys were placed in simulated space travel and given a general supply of food for a 30-day voyage. In the experiment, two monkeys died. The scientist who wrote the research report used these words in explaining one of the deaths: "One succumbed unexpectedly apparently as a result of an untoward response due to a change in feeding regimen." Because of the heavy language, we really do not learn what happened. Why did the writer not state clearly and simply like this: "One monkey died unexpectedly because he ate too much."?

Now, there is really nothing wrong with the hard words—if they are used intelligently. They are intelligently used when they are clearly understood by the reader, when they are best in conveying the meaning intended, and when they are used with wise moderation. Perhaps the best suggestion in this regard is to use words you would use in face-to-face communication with your reader. Another good suggestion is to use the simplest words which carry the thought without offending the reader's intelligence.

The communication advantages of familiar words over the far more complex ones is obvious from the following contrasting examples:

Formal and complex	*Familiar words*
The conclusion ascertained from a perusal of the pertinent data is that a lucrative market exists for the product.	The data studied show that the product is in good demand.
The antiquated mechanisms were utilized for the experimentation.	The old machines were used for the test.
Company operations for the preceding accounting period terminated with a substantial deficit.	The company lost much money last year.

Prefer the short to the long word. Because short words tend to communicate better than long ones, you should prefer them in your writing. As has been borne out by readability studies, a heavy proportion of long words confuses the reader. Some of the explanation is that the long words tend to be the more difficult ones. In addition, however, the readability studies indicate that long words give the appearance of being hard; thus, our minds receive them as hard words. The studies give evidence that even when the long words are understood, a heavy proportion of them adds to the difficulty of comprehension.

There are, of course, many exceptions to this rule. Some words like *hypnotize, hippopotamus,* and *automobile* are so well known that they communicate easily; and some short words like *verd, vie,* and *gybe* are understood by only a few. On the whole, however, word length and word difficulty are correlated. Thus, you will be wise to use long words with some caution. And you will need to be certain that the long ones you use are well known to your reader.

The following contrasting sentences clearly show the effect of long words on writing clarity. Most of the long words are likely to be understood by most educated readers, but the heavy proportion of long words makes for heavy reading and slow communication. Without question, the simple versions communicate better.

Heavy on long words	Short and simple words
A decision was *predicated* on the *assumption* that an abundance of *monetary* funds was *forthcoming*.	The decision was *based* on the *belief* that there would be *more* money.
They *acceded* to the *proposition* to *terminate* business.	They *agreed* to *quit* business.
During the *preceding* year the company *operated* at a *financial deficit*.	*Last* year the company *lost* money.
Prior to accelerating productive operation, the foreman inspected the machinery.	*Before speeding up production*, the foreman inspected the machinery.
Definitive action was *effected subsequent* to the reporting date.	Final action was *taken after* the reporting date.

Use technical words with caution. Whatever your field will be in business, it will have its own jargon. In time, this jargon will become a part of your everyday working vocabulary. So common will this jargon appear in your mental filter that you may assume that others outside the field also know it. And in writing to those outside your field, you may use these words. The result is miscommunication.

Certainly, it is logical to use the language of a field in writing to those in the field. But even in such instances you can overdo it, for an overuse of technical words can be hard reading even for technical people. Frequently, technical words are long and hard-sounding. As we noted in the preceding rule, such words tend to dull the writing and to make the writing hard to understand. Also, the difficulty tends to increase as the proportion of technical words increases. Illustrating this point is the following sentence written by a physician:

> It is a methodology error to attempt to interpret psychologically an organic symptom which is the end result of an intermediary change of organic processes instead of trying to understand those vegetative, nervous impulses in their relation to psychological factors which introduce a change of organic events resulting in an organic disturbance.

No doubt the length of this sentence contributes to its difficulty, but the heavy proportion of technical terms also makes understanding difficult. The conclusion that may be drawn here is obvious. When you write to your fellow technicians, you may use technical words, but you should use them moderately.

In writing to those outside the field, you should write in layman language. For example, a physician might well refer to a "cerebral vascular accident" in writing to a fellow physician, but he would do well to use the word *stroke* in writing to the layman. An accountant writing to a nonaccountant might also need to avoid the jargon of his profession. Even though terms like *accounts receivable, liabilities,* and *surplus* are elementary to him, they may be meaningless to some people. So, in writing to such people, he would be wise to use non-technical descriptions such as "how much is owed the company," "how much the company owes," and "how much was left over." Similar examples can be drawn from any specialized field.

Bringing the writing to life with words

As we noted in our analysis of the communication process, our sensory receptors and our minds do not give equal attention to all our perceptions. Some they completely ignore. Others they give varying degrees of attention, ranging from almost none to the strong and vigorous. Obviously, it is the strong and vigorous perceptions which communicate best.

Applied to written communication, this observation means that symbols which are strong and vigorous are more likely to gain and hold the interest of your reader. Subject matter is a major determinant of the interest quality of communication; but even interesting topics can be presented in writing so dull that an interested reader cannot keep his mind on the subject. If you wish to avoid this possibility, you will need to bring your writing to life with words.

Bringing your writing to life with words is no simple undertaking. In fact, it involves techniques which practically defy description—techniques which even the most accomplished writers never completely master. In spite of the difficulty of this undertaking, however, you can bring your writing to life by following four simple but important suggestions: (1) You can select strong and vigorous words, (2) you can use concrete words, (3) you can prefer active verbs, and (4) you can avoid overuse of the camouflaged verbs.

Use strong, vigorous words. Like people, words have personality. Some words are strong and vigorous, some are dull and weak, and others fall in between these extremes. In improving your writing skill, you should be aware of these differences whenever you write. You should become a student of words, and you should strive to select words which will produce just the right effect in your reader's mind. You should recognize, for example, that "tycoon" is stronger than "eminently successful businessman," that "bear market" is stronger than "generally declining market," and that a "boom" is stronger than a "period of business prosperity." As a rule, you should make the strong words predominate.

In selecting the strong word, you should be aware that the verb is the strongest part of speech, and it is closely followed by the noun. The verb is the action word, and action by its very nature commands interest. Nouns, of course, are the doers of action—the characters in the story, so to speak As doers of action, they attract the reader's attention.

Contrary to what you may think, adjectives and adverbs should be used sparingly. These words add length to the sentence, thereby distracting the reader's attention from the key nouns and verbs. As Voltaire phrased it, "The adjective is the enemy of the noun." In addition, adjectives and adverbs both involve subjective evaluation; and as previously noted, the objective approach is necessary in many forms of business communication.

Use the concrete word. Interesting business writing is marked by specific words—words which form sharp and clear meaning in your reader's brain. Such words are concrete. Concrete words are the opposite of abstract words, which are words of fuzzy and vague meaning. In general, concrete words stand for things the reader perceives—things he can see, feel, hear, taste, or smell. Concrete words hold interest, for they move directly into the reader's experience. Because concrete words are best for holding interest, you should prefer them to abstract words wherever possible.

To a large extent, concrete words are the short, familiar words previously discussed. They are the words at the bottom of the abstraction ladder—the words which make sharp, clear meanings in the mind. In addition to being more meaningful to your reader, such words generally have more precise meanings than the other words. For example, this sentence is filled with long, unfamiliar words: "The magnitude of the increment of profits was the predominant motivating factor in the decision." Written in shorter and more familiar words, the idea becomes more concrete: "The size of the profit gained was the chief reason for the decision."

Concreteness involves more than simplicity, for many of the well-known words are abstract. Perhaps we can make a clear distinction between concrete and abstract wording by illustration. In the write-up of the results of an experiment a chemist might refer to the bad odor of a certain mixture as a "nauseous odor." But these words do little to communicate a clear mental picture in the reader's mind, for *nauseous* is a word with many different meanings. Were the chemist to say that the substance smelled like "decaying fish," his words would be likely to communicate a clear meaning in the reader's mind. One of the best-known examples of concreteness is in the advertising claim that Ivory soap is "$99^{44}/_{100}$ percent pure." Had the company used abstract words such as "Ivory soap is very pure," few people would have been impressed. But the firm used specific words, and millions took notice. Similar differences in abstract and concrete expressions are apparent in the following:

Abstract	Concrete
A sizable profit	A 22 percent profit
Good accuracy	Pinpoint accuracy
The leading student	Top student in a class of 90
The majority	Fifty-three percent
In the near future	By Thursday noon
A work-saving machine	Does the work of 7 men
Easy to steer	Quick-steering
Light in weight	Featherlight

Prefer active to passive verbs. Of all the parts of speech, the verbs are the strongest, and verbs are at their strongest when they are in the active voice. Thus, for the best in vigorous, lively writing, you should make good use of active-voice verbs. Certainly, this suggestion does not mean that you should eliminate passive voice, for passive voice has a definite place in good writing, especially when you wish to give emphasis to words other than the verb. But it does mean that you should use as much active voice as you logically can.

Active-voice verbs are those which show their subject doing the action. They contrast with the dull, passive forms which act upon their subjects. The following contrasting sentences illustrate the distinction:

Active: The auditor inspected the books.
Passive: The books were inspected by the auditor.

The first example clearly is the stronger. In this sentence the doer of the action acts, and the verb is short and clear. In the second example, the helping word *were* dulls the verb, and the doer of the action is relegated to a role in a prepositional phrase. The following sentences give additional proof of the superiority of active over passive voice:

72

Passive	Active
The new process is believed to be superior by the investigators.	Investigators believe that the new process is superior.
The policy was enforced by the committee.	The committee enforced the policy.
The office will be inspected by Mr. Hall.	Mr. Hall will inspect the office.
A gain of 30.1 percent was recorded for Softlines sales.	Softlines sales gained 30.1 percent.
It is desired by this office that this problem be brought before the board.	This office desires that the secretary bring this problem before the board.
A complete reorganization of the administration was effected by the president.	The president completely reorganized the administration.

Avoid overuse of camouflaged verbs. Closely related to the problem of using abstract words and passive voice is the problem of camouflaged verbs. A verb is camouflaged when it appears in the sentence as an abstract noun rather than in verb form. For example, in the sentence "Elimination of the excess material was effected by the crew," the noun *elimination* is made out of the verb *eliminate*. Although there is nothing wrong with nouns made from verbs, in this case the noun form carries the strongest action idea of the sentence. A more vigorous phrasing would use the pure verb form, as in this example: "The crew eliminated the excess material." Likewise, it is stronger to "cancel" than to "effect a cancellation"; it is stronger to "consider" than to "give consideration to"; and it is stronger to "appraise" than to "make an appraisal." These sentences further illustrate the point:

Camouflaged verbs	Clear verb form
Amortization of the account was effected by the staff.	The staff amortized the account.
Control of the water was not possible.	They could not control the water.
The new policy involved the standardization of the procedures.	The new policy involved standardizing the procedures.
Application of the mixture was accomplished.	They applied the mixture.

From these illustrations and those of the preceding discussion of passive voice, two helpful writing rules may be gleaned. The first is to make the subjects of most sentences either persons or things. For example, rather than writing "Consideration was given to . . . ," you should write "We consider. . . ." The second rule is to write most sentences in normal (subject, verb, object) order, with the real doer of action as the subject. It is when you attempt other orders that you are most likely to produce involved, strained, passive structures.

Selecting words for precise communication

Good business writing requires some mastery of language—enough, at least, to enable the writer to communicate with reasonable accuracy. Unfortunately, all too often we select words as a matter of routine. We select words without carefully thinking out the meanings they will bring to the mind of our reader. Sometimes we even use words we do not understand. The result is writing which is as vague and fuzzy as our process of word selection.

Even though our words do not convey precise meanings, we can use them with much more precision than we do. We should all do a better job of learning more of the accepted uses of each word. Especially should we learn the shades of differences in the meanings of similar words and the different meanings various arrangements of words can bring about. For example, you must learn that the word *fewer* pertains to smaller numbers of units or individuals and that the word *less* relates to value, degree, or quantity. You must know the differences in connotation of similar words such as *secondhand, used,* and *antique; slender, thin,* and *skinny; suggest, tell,* and *inform; tramp, hobo,* and *vagabond.*

CONSTRUCTION OF SENTENCES WHICH COMMUNICATE

Arranging your words into sentences which form meaning in your reader's mind is a major part of your task as a business writer. As with using words, this task is one of adaptation—of fitting the message to a particular reader or readers.

Largely, your task of adapting sentences to your reader is a mental one. On the one hand, you visualize your reader; on the other, you structure words into sentences which produce the intended meaning in his mind. In structuring your words, you are guided by your own best judgment, for constructing sentences clearly is a product of the thinking mind. The sentence is a form man has devised to express his thought units. Thus, clear and orderly sentences are the product of clear and orderly thinking; vague and disorderly sentences represent vague and disorderly thinking.

The technique of good thinking cannot be reduced to routine steps, procedures, formulas, or the like, for the process is too little understood. But sentences which are the product of good thinking do have clearly discernible characteristics. These characteristics suggest the general guidelines for good sentence construction which appear in the following paragraphs.

Keeping sentences short

More than any other characteristic of a sentence, length is most clearly related to sentence difficulty. The longer a sentence is, the harder it is to understand. This relationship is convincingly borne out by the readability studies previously cited. And it is a logical conclusion which we may draw from an analysis of the operation of the mind. We all know that our minds have limitations. We know that they are limited in their abilities to handle complex information. Some minds, of course, can handle more complex information than others, but they all have their maximum limit.

Complexity in communicating with words is largely determined by the number of relationships and the volume of information expressed in the sentence. When an excess of information or excessive relationships are presented in a single package, our minds have to work hard to grasp the message. In written communication, a repeated reading may be needed; and in the more extreme cases, even these may not produce results. Thus, like food, information is best consumed in bite sizes.

What is bite-size for the mind, however, depends on the mental capacity of the reader. Most of the readability studies conclude that writing aimed at the middle level of adult American readers should have an average sentence length of around 16 to 18 words. For more advanced readers the average can be higher. It must be lower for those of lower reading abilities. Of course, these length figures do not mean that short sentences of six or so words are taboo, nor do they mean that one should avoid long sentences of 30 or more words. Occasionally, short sentences may be used to emphasize an important fact, and long sentences may be skillfully constructed to subordinate some less important information. It is the average which should be in keeping with the readability level of the reader.

Differences brought about by sentence length are emphatically illustrated by the following contrasting sentences. Notice how much better the shorter versions communicate.

Long and hard to understand	*Short and clear*
Some authorities in personnel administration object to expanding normal salary ranges to include a trainee rate because they fear that probationers may be kept at the minimum rate longer than is warranted through oversight or prejudice and because they fear that it would encourage the spread from the minimum to maximum rate range.	Some authorities in personnel administration object to expanding the normal salary range to include a trainee rate for two reasons. First, they fear that probationers may be kept at the minimum rate longer than is warranted, through oversight or prejudice. Second, they fear that it would, in effect, increase the spread from the minimum to the maximum rate range.
Regardless of their seniority or union affiliation, all employees who hope to be promoted are expected to continue their education either by enrolling in the special courses to be offered by the company, which are scheduled to be given after working hours beginning next Wednesday, or by taking approved correspondence courses selected from a list which may be seen in the training office.	Regardless of their seniority or union affiliation, all employees who hope to be promoted are expected to continue their education in either of two ways. (1) They may enroll in special courses to be given by the company. (2) They may take approved correspondence courses selected from the list which may be seen in the training office.
Analyses of all the facts lead to the singular conclusion that the climatological conditions during the morning of December 15 constitute the only significant and documented deviation from what is a normal condition at this plant and that these unusual atmospheric conditions, combined with the ever present caustic mist originating from both Bayer and White Hydrate Precipitator areas, created a condition which appears to have	The facts point to one conclusion. Unusual atmospheric conditions on the morning of December 15 were the only deviations from normal. Apparently, these atmospheric conditions combined with the normal presence of caustic mist at the plant damaged the paint on the automobiles.

Long and hard to understand	*Short and clear*
been attributable to the destructive effects observed on the paint of the automobiles in question.	
When an employee has changed from job to another job the new corresponding coverages will be effective as of the date the change occurred, provided, however, if due to a physical disability or infirmity as a result of advanced age, an employee is changed from one job to another job and such change results in the employee's new job rate coming within a lower hourly job rate bracket in the table, the employee may, at the discretion of the company, continue the amount of group term life insurance and the amount of accidental death and dismemberment insurance which the employee had prior to such change.	When an employee changes jobs, his new insurance coverage becomes effective the day the change occurs. Exception may be made when the job change results from physical disability or advanced age and reduces the employee's hourly wages. In such cases, employee may, at the company's discretion, keep the coverage he had before the change.

Using words economically

Of the many ways in which every thought may be expressed, the shorter ways are usually the best. In general, the shorter wordings save the reader time; they are clearer; and they make for more vigorous and interesting reading. Thus, you should strive for economy in the use of words.

Learning to use words economically is a matter of continuing effort. You should continuously be aware of the need for word economy. You should carefully explore and appraise the many ways of expressing each thought. You should know that the possibility of word economy depends on the subject matter in each case. You should know also that there are certain ways of expression which simply are not economical. These you should avoid.

For the most part, writing economically means writing and rewriting to find the best possible wording. It involves cutting out unnecessary words and information. For example, take this somewhat awkward and loosely written sentence from a certain company's policy manual:

If an extra board employee is the senior man on the current transfer list for a regular vacancy when the vacancy occurs and has the necessary qualifications and the ability to perform in accordance with the job requirements, he will be transferred to that job.

With a bit of thought and effort, this more economical version might emerge:

Extra board employees will be transferred to fill a regular vacancy on the basis of seniority and qualification for the job.

In addition to generally policing your writing to achieve economy, you can keep in mind certain practices that tend to make our writing not concise. The most common of these appear in the following paragraphs.

Cluttering phrases. Our language is cluttered with numerous phrases which are best replaced by shorter expressions. Although the shorter forms may save only a word or two here and there, the little savings over a long piece of writing can be significant. As the following sentences illustrate, the shorter substitutes are better.

The long way	*Short and improved*
In the event that payment is not made by January, operations will cease.	If payment is not made by January, operations will cease.
In spite of the fact that they received help, they failed to exceed the quota.	*Even though* they received help, they failed to exceed the quota.
The invoice was *in the amount of* $50,000.	The invoice was *for* $50,000.

Here are other contrasting pairs of expressions:

Long	*Short*
Along the lines of	Like
For the purpose of	For
For the reason that	Because, since
In the near future	Soon
In accordance with	By
In very few cases	Seldom
In view of the fact that	Since, because
On the occasion of	On
With regard to, with reference to	About

Surplus words. You should eliminate words which add nothing to the sentence meaning. In some instances, however, eliminating the words requires recasting the sentence, as some of the following examples illustrate:

Contains surplus words	Surplus words eliminated
He ordered desks *which are of the* executive type.	He ordered executive-type desks.
It will be noted that the records for the past years show a steady increase in special appropriations.	The records for past years show a steady increase in special appropriations.
There are four rules *which* should be observed.	Four rules should be observed.
In addition to these defects, numerous other defects mar the operating procedure.	Numerous other defects mar the operating procedure.
His performance was good enough to *enable him to* qualify him for the promotion.	His performance was good enough to qualify him for promotion.
The machines *which were* damaged by the fire were repaired.	The machines damaged by the fire were repaired.
By *the* keeping *of* production records, they found the error.	By keeping production records, they found the error.

Roundabout construction. Of the many ways of saying anything some are direct and to the point; others cover the same ground in a roundabout way. Without question, the direct ways are usually better, and you should use them. Although there are many forms of roundabout expressions (some of them overlap the preceding causes of excess wording), the following illustrations clearly show the general nature of this violation:

Roundabout	Direct and to the point
The department budget *can be observed to be decreasing* each new year.	The department budget *decreases* each year.
The union is *involved in the task of reviewing* the seniority provision of the contract.	The union is *reviewing* the seniority provision of the contract.
The president is *of the opinion that* the tax was paid.	The president *believes* the tax was paid.
It is essential that the income be used to retire the debt.	The income *must* be used to retire the debt.
It is the committee's assumption that the evidence has been gathered.	The committee *assumes* that the evidence has been gathered.

Roundabout	*Direct and to the point*
The supervisors should *take appropriate action to determine* whether the timecards are being inspected.	The supervisors *should determine* whether the timecards are being inspected.
The price increase will *afford* the company *an opportunity* to retire the debt.	A price increase will *enable* the company to retire the debt.
During the time she was employed by this company, Miss Carr was absent once.	*While* employed by this company, Miss Carr was absent once.
He criticized everyone he *came in contact with.*	He criticized everyone he *met.*

Unnecessary repetition. You should work to avoid unnecessary repetition of words or thoughts. Exception to this rule, however, is justified when you wish to repeat for special effect or for emphasis.

Needless repetition	*Repetition eliminated*
The provision of Section 5 provides for a union shop.	Section 5 provides for a union shop.
The assignment of training the ineffective worker is *an assignment* we must carry out.	Training the ineffective worker is an assignment we must carry out.
Modern up-to-date equipment will be used.	Modern equipment will be used.
In the office they found supplies *there* which had never been issued.	In the office they found supplies which had never been issued.
He reported for work Friday *morning* at *8 a.m.*	He reported for work Friday at 8 a.m.
In my opinion I think the plan is sound.	I think the plan is sound.
The *important essentials* must not be neglected.	The essentials must not be neglected.

Considering emphasis in sentence design

All of the information you present in a report is not equally important to your message. Some subject matter, such as conclusions to reports or objectives of letters, plays a major role. On the other hand, some subject matter plays a supporting role—sometimes even an incidental one. A part of your task as a business writer is to determine the importance of each bit of information you present, and then to communicate this importance in your finished manuscript.

By doing this you exercise some control over the information your reader's mind receives. Thus, you are more likely to communicate. As we shall see later in our study, you may give emphasis to information in a number of ways. The one way of concern to us now is by sentence design.

Short, simple sentences carry more emphasis than do long, more involved sentences. Short sentences stand out and call attention to their content. The mind gets the message without the interference of related or supporting information. Especially you can gain emphasis with short sentences when you place them in positions of emphasis such as the beginnings and endings of paragraphs. As we shall soon see, such positions call attention to the subject matter concerned.

Sentences which cover two or more items give less emphasis to the content. Within these sentences, varying emphasis may be given each item. Those items placed in independent clauses get major emphasis. Those placed in subordinate structures (dependent clauses, parenthetic structures, modifiers, and the like) are relegated to less important roles. Thus, by skillful design, or by a lack of it, you may present the same facts in distinctly different ways, as shown by the following illustrations.

In the first illustration, separate sentences are used to present each item of information. Each item gets special emphasis by this treatment; but because all are treated the same, none stand out. Also, the items obviously are not equally important and should not be given equal emphasis. In addition, the writing is elementary to the point of being ridiculous.

> The main building was inspected on October 1. Mr. George Wills inspected the building. Mr. Wills is a vice president of the company. He found that the building has 6,500 square feet of floor space. He also found that it has 2,400 square feet of storage space. The new store must have a minimum of 6,000 square feet of floor space. It must have 2,000 square feet of storage space. Thus, the main building exceeds the space requirements for the new store. Therefore, Mr. Wills concluded that the main building is adequate for the company's needs.

In the next illustration, some of the information is subordinated, but not logically. The facts of real importance do not receive the emphasis they deserve. Logically, the points that should be emphasized are the conclusions that the building is large enough and the supporting evidence showing that floor and storage space exceeds minimum requirements.

Mr. George Wills, who inspected the main building on October 1, is a vice president of the company. His inspection, which supports the conclusion that the building is large enough for the proposed store, uncovered these facts. The store has 6,500 square feet of floor space and 2,400 square feet of storage space, which is more than the minimum requirement of 6,000 and 2,000 square feet, respectively, of floor and storage space.

The next illustration gives good emphasis to the pertinent points. The short, simple sentences placed for emphasis at the beginning present the conclusion. The supporting facts that the new building exceeds the minimum of floor and storage space requirements receive main-clause emphasis. Incidentals such as the identifying remarks about George Wills are relegated to subordinate roles.

The main building is large enough for the new store. This conclusion, made by Vice President George Wills following his October 1 inspection of the building, is based on these facts: The building's 6,500 square feet of floor space are 500 more than the 6,000 set as the minimum. The 2,400 square feet of storage space are 400 more than the 2,000 minimum requirement.

More specific violations of logical emphasis are illustrated in the following sentences. The first shows how placing an important idea in an appositional construction weakens the idea. Notice the increased emphasis given the idea (by position and by construction) in the second sentence.

Weak emphasis: Hamilton's typewriter, a machine which has been used daily for almost 40 years, is in good condition.
Strong emphasis: Although Hamilton's typewriter has been used daily for 40 years, it is in good condition.

The next sentence shows how an idea may be subordinated through placement in a particular construction. The idea receives more emphasis as a dependent clause in the second sentence.

Weak emphasis: Having paid the highest dividend in its history, the company anticipates a rise in the value of its stock.
Strong emphasis: Because it has paid the highest dividend in its history, the company anticipates a rise in the value of its stock.

Arranging sentences for clarity

Words alone do not make a message, for their arrangement also plays a role in the meanings given by our minds. All languages have certain rules of arrangement which help to determine meaning. These rules are generally fixed in our minds, and they are a part of our filter operation. Thus, to violate them is to invite miscommunication.

The rules of our language have been thoroughly cataloged by scholars of the past, and all of us have been exposed to them in our study of language. Contrary to what many of us may think, these rules of language are not merely arbitrary requirements set by detail-minded scholars. Rather, the rules are statements of logical relationships between words. Dangling participles, for example, confuse meaning by modifying the wrong words. Unparallel constructions leave erroneous impressions of the parts. Pronouns without clear antecedents have no definite meaning. The evidence is quite clear: The business writer must know and follow the conventional standards of his language.

Unfortunately, too many of us know too little about the conventional rules of English grammar. Why so many people have resisted this subject through years of drill at all levels of education is a mystery to educators. Obviously, the area is too broad for complete coverage in this book. Some of the points with which most of us have trouble, however, are presented for quick review in Chapter 6. You should not ignore their importance.

CARE IN PARAGRAPH DESIGN

In writing, we do not communicate by words and sentences alone. Paragraphs also play a major role. As we shall see, how a paragraph is designed helps to organize it as it goes into our mind. In addition, the rest stop provided by paragraphing gives a psychological if not real boost to our receptiveness to messages.

How we should go about designing paragraphs is not easily put into words. Much of paragraph writing depends on the writer's mental ability to organize and to relate facts logically. Thus, it is a mental process about which we know little. There are, however, some general suggestions you would be wise to follow. They are summarized for you in the following paragraphs.

Giving the paragraph unity

A first suggestion in paragraph design is to give the paragraph unity. Unity, of course, means oneness. When applied to paragraph construction, it means that you should build the paragraph around a single topic or idea. That is, you should include only this major topic or idea plus the supporting details which help to develop it. Exceptions to the rule of unity are the transitional paragraphs whose objectives are to relate preceding and succeeding topics.

Just what constitutes unity is not always easy to determine. All of a report, for example, may deal with a single topic and therefore unity. The same could be said for each major division of the report as well as for the lesser subdivisions. Paragraph unity, however, concerns smaller units than these—usually the lowest level of a detailed outline. That is, in reports written with detailed outlines, each paragraph might well cover one of the lowest outline captions. In any event, one good test of a paragraph is to reduce its content to a single topic statement. If this statement does not cover the paragraph content, unity is not likely to be there.

Keeping the paragraphs short

In most forms of business writing, you would be wise to keep your paragraphs short. Short paragraphs help your reader to follow the organizational plan of the paper. Specifically, they help him to see the beginning and ending of each item covered, and they give added emphasis to the facts covered. In addition, short paragraphs are more inviting to the eye. People simply prefer to read material which gives them frequent breaks. This is true so long as the breaks are not too frequent. A series of very short paragraphs would leave an equally offensive choppy effect.

A glance at Figure 5-1 quickly shows the psychological effect of paragraph length. The full page of solid type appears to be more difficult and generally less inviting than the one marked by short paragraphs. Even if both contained exactly the same words, the difference would be present. Perhaps this difference is largely psychological. Psychological or not, it is real.

Just how long a paragraph should be is, of course, dependent upon the topic. Some topics are short; others are long; still others are in between. Even so, a general rule can be given as to paragraph length. Most well-organized and well-paragraphed business papers have paragraphs averaging around eight or nine lines. Some good paragraphs may be quite short—even a single sentence. And some may be well over the eight-to-nine-line average.

84

FIGURE 5-1
Contrasting pages showing psychological effects of long and short paragraphs

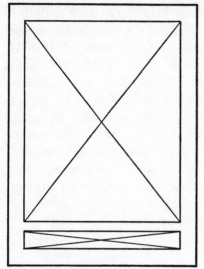

Heavy paragraphs make the
writing appear to be dull
and difficult.

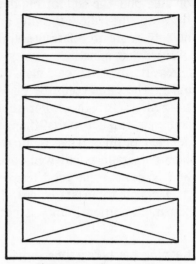

Short paragraphs give well
organized effect—invite the
reader to read.

One good rule of thumb to follow is to question the unity of all long paragraphs—say those exceeding 12 lines. If inspection shows you that only one topic is present, you should make no change. But if the paragraph covers more than one topic, you should make additional paragraphs.

Putting topic sentences to good use

In organizing your paragraphs, you will need to make effective use of the topic sentence. A topic sentence, of course, is the sentence in a paragraph which expresses the main idea of a paragraph. Around this topic sentence, the details which support or elaborate the main idea build in some logical way. Exactly how a given paragraph should build from the topic sentence largely depends on the information to be covered and on the writer's plan in covering it. Obviously, much of paragraph design must come from your mental effort. You would profit, however, by being generally acquainted with the paragraph plans most commonly used.

Topic sentence first. The most widely used paragraph plan begins with the topic sentence. The supporting material then follows in some logical order. As this arrangement gives good emphasis to the major point, it will be the most useful to you as a business writer. In fact, some company manuals suggest that this arrangement be used almost altogether. As the following paragraph illustrates, this arrangement has merit.

Illustration

A majority of the economists consulted think that business activity will drop during the first quarter of next year. Of the 185 economists interviewed, 13 percent looked for continued increases in business activities; and 28 percent anticipated little or no change from the present high level. The remaining 59 percent looked for a recession. Of this group, nearly all (87 percent) believed the down curve would occur during the first quarter of the year.

Topic sentence at end.   Another logical paragraph arrangement places the topic sentence at the end, usually as a conclusion. The supporting details come first and in logical order build toward the topic sentence. Frequently, such paragraphs use a beginning sentence to set up or introduce the subject, as in the following illustration. Such a sentence serves as a form of topic sentence, but the real meat of the paragraph is covered in the final sentence.

Illustration

The significant role of inventories in the economic picture should not be overlooked. At present, inventories represent 3.8 months supply. Their dollar value is the highest in history. If considered in relation to increased sales, however, they are not excessive. In fact, they are well within the range generally believed to be safe. *Thus, inventories are not likely to cause a downward swing in the economy.*

Topic sentences within the paragraph.   Some paragraphs are logically arranged with the topic sentence somewhere within. These paragraphs are not often used, and usually for good reason. In general, they fail to give proper emphasis to the key points in the paragraph. Even so, they may sometimes be used with good effect, as in this example:

Illustration

Numerous materials have been used in manufacturing this part. And many have shown quite satisfactory results. *Material 329, however, is superior to them all.* Built with material 329, the part is almost twice as strong as when built with the next best material. Also, it is three ounces lighter. And most important, it is cheaper than any of the other products.

Making the paragraph move forward

Each paragraph you write should clearly move an additional step toward your objective. Such forward movement is a good quality of paragraph design. Individual sentences have little movement, for they cover only a single thought. An orderly succession of single thoughts, however, does produce movement. In addition, good movement is helped by skillful use of transition, by smoothness in writing style, and by a general proficiency in word choice and sentence design.

Perhaps the quality of movement is easier to see than to describe. In general, it is present when the reader is made to feel at the paragraph end that he had made one sure step toward the objective. Although many arrangements can illustrate good paragraph movement, the following does the job exceptionally well:

> First, building rock in the Crowton area is questionable. The failure of recent geological explorations in the area appears to confirm suspicions that the Crowton deposits are nearly exhausted. Second, distances from Crowton to major consumption areas make transportation costs unusually high. Obviously, any savings in transportation costs will add to company profits. Third, obsolescence of much of the equipment at the Crowton plant makes this an ideal time for relocation. New equipment could be moved directly to the new site, and obsolete equipment could be scrapped in the Crowton area.

A WORD OF CAUTION

Like most elements of writing, the foregoing principles must be tempered with good judgment. If followed blindly to an extreme degree, they can produce writing which takes on the appearance of being mechanical or which in some way calls attention to writing style rather than to content. For example, slavish application of the rules for short sentences could produce a primer style of writing. So could the rules stressing simple language. Such writing could be offensive to the more sophisticated reader. Your solution is to use the rules as general guides, but clear and logical thinking must guide you in your use of them.

6

Correctness in writing

Correctness in grammar and punctuation are additional contributors to the clarity of your writing. This is not to say that incorrect wording cannot communicate. The semiliterate person who writes "I ain't never seen no need for no grammar," gets his message across in spite of the excessive negatives. And most of the time missing a punctuation mark here and there has little effect on the basic message. But occasionally there are exceptions when incorrect punctuation causes a communication error. For example, placement of a comma in this table title does much to determine its meaning: "Population of California, Broken Down by Age and Sex." Now read it without the comma. The only way to avoid such errors is to write correctly at all times.

In addition to writing correctly to avoid communication error, you will want to write correctly for personal reasons. Writing errors are not likely to go undetected. They stand out like sore thumbs to those who know correctness. Obviously, you draw the blame for such errors. So, as a matter of pride, you should want to avoid making them. Unfortunately, correctness is not always a clear-cut matter. As you may know, in recent years there has been a general relaxation of the traditional rules of punctuation and grammar. Communication of the message has emerged as a primary consideration, with correctness being of value mainly to the extent it helps to communicate.

Such reasoning is hard to quarrel with. Certainly, communication should be the primary goal of writing; and so many of the traditional rules of grammar and punctuation are so very arbitrary. For example, the conventional rule against splitting infinitives has little justification for communication effectiveness. For another, the rule of not ending a sentence with a preposition runs contrary to our conversational practice. Perhaps Winston Churchill put this one to rest with his classic comment: "This is one rule up with which I will not put."

Our approach to reviewing the subject of correctness is to cover mainly those standards that are most likely to affect communication clarity. First, we shall review the major means of achieving clarity through punctuation; then we shall do likewise for grammar. Should you feel the need to follow some of the lesser rules for correctness, you may consult any of a number of comprehensive handbooks on the subject. For your convenience in finding particular standards, they are arranged alphabetically and grouped by basic types.

STANDARDS FOR PUNCTUATION

Apostrophe

1. The possessive case of nouns and indefinite pronouns is shown by the use of the apostrophe. If the nominative form of the word concerned does not end in *s*, an apostrophe and an *s* are added. But if the word does end in *s*, only an apostrophe is added.

Nominative form	Possessive form
company	company's
employee	employee's
companies	companies'
employees	employees'

Proper names and singular nouns which end in *s* sounds, however, are exceptions to this practice. Such words add the apostrophe and the *s* to the nominative singular; to the nominative plural only an apostrophe is added.

Nominative form	Possessive form
Texas (singular)	Texas's
Joneses (plural)	Joneses'
Jones (singular)	Jones's
countess (singular)	countess's

2. The place in a contraction where letters are omitted is marked with the apostrophe.

has not = hasn't
cannot = can't
it is = it's

3. The apostrophe is used in the plural of letters, numbers, and words considered merely as words.

Examples

There were three *17's* recorded in the final tabulation.

The first list ended with the *k's*.

If you are to achieve the conversational tone, you must use more *I's* and *you's* in your writing.

Brackets

Brackets are used to set off words which the author wishes to insert in a quotation. (With the typewriter the left bracket is made by striking the diagonal, backspacing once, striking the underscore, rolling the platen up a line space, and striking the underscore again.)

Examples

"Possibly the use of this type of supervisor [the trained correspondence expert] is still on the increase."

"At least direct supervision has gained in importance in the past decade [the report was written in 1961], during which time 43 percent of the reporting business firms that started programs have used this technique."

Colon

1. The colon is used to introduce a statement of explanation, an enumeration, or a formal quotation.

Examples

Statement of explanation: At this time the company was pioneering a new marketing idea: It was attempting to sell its products directly to consumers by means of vending machines.

Enumeration: There are four classes of machinists working in this department: apprentice machinist, journeyman machinist, machinist, and first-class machinist.

Formal quotation: President Hartung had this to say about the proposal: "Any such movement which fails to have the support of the rank-and-file worker in this plant fails to get my support."

2. The colon should not be used when the thought of the sentence should continue without interruption. If it is a list that is being introduced by a colon, the list should be in apposition to a preceding word.

Examples

Below standard: Cities in which new sales offices are in operation are: Fort Smith, Texarkana, Lake Charles, Jackson, and Biloxi.

Acceptable: Cities in which new sales offices are in operation are Fort Smith, Texarkana, Lake Charles, Jackson, and Biloxi.

Acceptable: Cities in which new sales offices are in operation are as follows: Fort Smith, Texarkana, Lake Charles, Jackson, and Biloxi.

3. Words or phrases that introduce lists, such as *namely, that is, for example,* or *i.e.,* are preceded by the colon and followed by the comma if the lists are clauses or long phrases. But a lighter mark—a dash or a comma—may precede the listing word introducing a single item.

Example

There is a man among us, namely Mark, who can fill the bill.

Comma

1. Principal clauses connected by a coordinating conjunction are separated by a comma. The coordinating conjunctions are *and, but, or, nor,* and *for.*

Examples

Only two of the components of the index declined, and these two account for only 12 percent of the total weight of the index.

New automobiles are moving at record volumes, but used-car sales are lagging well behind the record pace set two years ago.

Exceptions may be made to this rule, however, in the case of compound sentences consisting of short and closely connected clauses.

Examples

We sold and the price dropped.

Sometimes we profit and sometimes we lose.

2.1. Elements listed in series should be set apart by commas. In order to avoid misinterpretation in rare instances when some of the elements listed have compound constructions, it is best to place the comma between the last two items (before the final conjunction).

Examples

Good copy must cover facts with accuracy, sincerity, honesty, and conviction.

Direct advertising can be used to introduce salesmen, fill in between salesmen's calls, cover territory where salesmen cannot be maintained, and keep pertinent reference material in the hands of prospects.

A survey conducted at the 1974 automobile show indicated that black and cream, blue and grey, dark maroon, and black cars were favored by the public. (Note how this example illustrates the need for a comma before the final conjunction.)

2.2. Coordinate adjectives in series are separated by commas when they modify the same noun and if there is no *and* connecting them. A good test to determine whether adjectives are coordinate is to insert an *and* between the words. If the *and* does not change the meaning of the expression, the words are coordinate.

Examples

Miss Pratt has been a reliable, faithful, efficient employee for 20 years.

We guarantee that this is a good, clean car.

Light green office furniture is Mr. Orr's recommendation for the stenographic pool. [If *and* were placed between *light* and *green,* the word meaning would be changed.]

A big Dawson wrench proved to be best for the task. [The *and* won't fit between *big* and *Dawson.*]

3.1. A nonrestrictive modifier is set off from the sentence by commas. By a nonrestrictive modifier is meant a modifier which could be omitted from the sentence without changing the meaning of the sentence. Restrictive modifiers (those which restrict the words they modify to one particular object) are not set off by commas. A restrictive modifier cannot be left out of the sentence without changing the sentence meaning.

Examples

Restrictive: The salesman who sells the most will get a bonus. [*Who sells the most* restricts the meaning to one particular salesman.]

Nonrestrictive: James Smithers, who was the company's top salesman for the year, was awarded a bonus. [If the clause *who was the company's top salesman for the year* is omitted, the statement is not changed.]

Restrictive: J. Ward & Company is the firm which employs most of the physically handicapped in this area.

Nonrestrictive: J. Ward & Company, the firm which employs most of the physically handicapped in this area, has gained the admiration of the community.

Notice how some sentences could be either restrictive or non-restrictive, depending on the meaning intended by the writer.

Examples

Restrictive: All of the suits which were damaged in the fire were sold at a discount. [Implies that a part of the stock was not damaged.]

Nonrestrictive: All of the suits, which were damaged by the fire, were sold at a discount. [Implies that all the stock was damaged.]

3.2. Note that *as* and *since* in their original use as time words introduce restrictive clauses and take no punctuation, but in their derived use as cause words they introduce added or nonrestrictive clauses, which require comma punctuation.

Examples

Restrictive–time: I have not seen him since he returned.

Nonrestrictive–cause or reason: I shall see him Tuesday, as we shall meet at Rotary.

4.1. Parenthetic expressions are set off by commas. A parenthetic expression consists of words which interrupt the normal flow of the sentence. In a sense, they appear to be "stuck in." In many instances they are simply words out of normal order. For example, the sentence "A full-page, black-and-white advertisement was run in the *Daily Bulletin*" contains a parenthetic expression when the word order is altered: "An advertisement, full-page and in black and white, was run in the *Daily Bulletin.*"

Examples

This practice, it is believed, will lead to ruin.

The Johnston Oil Company, so the rumor goes, has cut back sharply its exploration activity.

Although the dash and the parentheses may also be used for similar reasons, the three marks differ as to the degree to which they separate the enclosed words from the rest of the sentence. The comma is the weakest of the three, and it is best used when the material set off is closely related to the surrounding words. Dashes are stronger marks than commas and are used when the words set off tend to be long or contain internal punctuation marks. Parentheses, the strongest of the three, are primarily used to enclose material which helps to explain or supplement the main words of the sentence.

4.2. A comma is used to set off an appositive (a noun or a noun and its modifiers inserted to explain another noun) from the rest of the sentence. In a sense, appositives are forms of parenthetic expressions, for they do interrupt the normal flow of the sentence.

Examples

The Baron Corporation, our machine-parts supplier, is negotiating a new contract.

St. Louis, home office of our midwest district, will be the permanent site of our annual sales meeting.

President Carthwright, a self-educated man, is the leading advocate of our night school for employees.

But appositives which identify very closely are not set off by commas.

Examples

The word *liabilities* is not understood by most laboring men.

Our next shipment will come on the steamship *Alberta.*

4.3. Commas are used to set off parenthetic words such as *therefore, however, in fact, of course, for example,* and *consequently.*

Examples

It is apparent, therefore, that the buyers' resistance has been brought about by an overvigorous sales campaign.

After the first experiment, for example, the traffic flow increased 10 percent.

The company will, however, be forced to abandon the old pricing system.

Included in this group of introductory words may be interjections (*oh, alas*) and responsive expressions (*yes, no, surely, indeed, well,* and others). But if the words are strongly exclamatory or are not closely connected with the rest of the sentence, they may be punctuated as a sentence. *(No. Yes. Indeed.)*

94

Examples

Yes, the decision to increase production has been made.

Oh, contribute whatever you think is adequate.

4.4. When more than one unit appears in a date or an address, the units are set off by commas.

Examples

One unit: December 30 is the date of our annual inventory.

One unit: The company has one outlet in Ohio.

More than one unit: December 30, 1906, is the date the Johnston Company first opened its doors.

More than one unit: Richmond, Virginia, is the headquarters of the new sales district.

5.1. Subordinate clauses which precede main clauses are usually set off by commas.

Examples

Although it is durable, this package does not have eye appeal.

Since there was little store traffic on aisle 13, the area was converted into office space.

5.2. Introductory verbal phrases usually are followed by a comma. A verbal phrase is one which contains some verb derivative—a gerund, a participle, or an infinitive.

Examples

Participle phrase: Realizing his mistake, the foreman instructed his men to keep a record of all salvaged equipment.

Gerund phrase: After gaining the advantage, we failed to press on to victory.

Infinitive phrase: To increase our turnover of automobile accessories, we must first improve our display area.

6.1.1. The comma is used only for good reason. It is not a mark to be inserted indiscriminately at the whims of the writer. As a rule, use of commas should always be justified by one of the standard practices previously noted.

6.1.2. Do not be tripped into putting a comma between subject and verb.

Example

The thought that he could not afford to fail spurred him on. [No comma after *fail*.]

6.1.3. Ordinarily, do not set off the second element of a compound predicate with a comma. (The compound predicate is usually a weak and unemphatic structure and needs recasting instead of bolstering with an apologetic comma.)

6.2. The only exception to the preceding notes should be in instances where clarity of expression may be helped by the insertion of a comma.

Examples

Not clear: From the beginning inventory methods of Hill Company have been haphazard.

Clear: From the beginning, inventory methods of Hill Company have been haphazard.

Dash

The dash may be used to set off an element for emphasis or to show interrupted thought. Particularly is it used with long parenthetic expressions or those containing internal punctuation. With the typewriter, the dash is made by striking the hyphen twice, without spacing before or after.

Examples

Budgets for some past years—1971, for example—were prepared without consulting the department heads.

The test proved that the new process is simple, effective, accurate—and more expensive.

Only one person—the foreman in charge—has authority to issue such an order.

If you want a voice in the government—vote.

Exclamation point

The exclamation point is used at the end of a sentence or an exclamatory fragment to show strong emotion. This mark should be used sparingly; never should it be used with trivial ideas.

Examples

We've done it again!
No! It can't be!

Hyphen

1. Division of a word at the end of a line is indicated by the hyphen. The division must be made between syllables. It is generally impractical to leave a one-letter syllable at the end of a line *(a-bove)* or to carry over a two-letter syllable to the next line *(expens-es)*.

2.1. Hyphens are placed between the parts of some compound words. Generally, the hyphen is used whenever its absence would confuse the meaning of the words.

Examples

Compound nouns: brother-in-law, cure-all, city-state.

Compound numbers under 100 and above 20: thirty-one, fifty-five, seventy-seven.

Compound adjectives (two or more words used before a noun as a single adjective): *long-term* contract, *50-gallon* drum, *door-to-door* selling, *end-of-month* clearance.

Prefixes (most have been absorbed into the word): de-emphasize, ex-chairman, vice-chairman, anti-intellectual.

2.2. A proper name used as a compound adjective needs no hyphen or hyphens to hold it together as a visual unit for the reader: The capitals perform that function.

Examples

Correct: A Lamar High School student
Correct: A United Airlines pilot

2.3. Two or more modifiers in normal grammatical form and order need no hyphens. Particularly, a phrase consisting of an unmistakable adverb (one ending in *ly*) modifying an adjective or participle which in turn modifies a noun shows normal grammatical order and is readily grasped by the reader without the aid of the hyphen. But an adverb not ending in *ly* had better be joined to its adjectives or participle by the hyphen.

Examples

No hyphen needed: A poorly drawn chart
Use the hyphen: A well-prepared chart

Italics

1. For the use of italics to set out book titles, see Question

mark 4. Note that this device is also used to set out names of periodicals, of works of art or music, and of naval vessels and aircraft.

2. Foreign words and abbreviations thereof should be italicized—if you must use them. Italicize standard foreign (usually Latin) words and abbreviations used in footnotes and book references. This list includes *circa, c.* ("about"); *et al.* ("and others"); *ibidem, ibid.* ("in the same place"); *idem* ("the same"); *infra* ("below"); *supra* ("above"); *loco citato, loc. cit.* ("in the place cited"); *opere citato, op. cit.* ("in the work cited"); *passim* ("here and there"); *sic* ("so," "thus"); *quod vide, q.v.* ("which see"). But the commonly used "versus," or "vs.," or "v." has become anglicized and needs no underscoring.

3. Italicizing a word, letter, or figure used as its own name, or as a physical unit instead of a symbol of an idea, is a prime requisite for clearness. Without this device, we could not write this set of rules. Note the use of italics all through to label name words.

Examples

The little word *sell* is still in the dictionary.

The pronoun *which* should always have a noun as a clear antecedent. [Try reading that one without the italics: It becomes a fragment ending in mid air!]

4. If your entire passage is already italicized or underlined (as in the case of a caption underlined for emphasis), how should you distinguish a title, a foreign word, or a word normally italicized? Your best resort is to shift back to the roman type, or in typing to *omit* the underline.

Parentheses

Parentheses may be used to set off words which are parenthetic or which are inserted to explain or to supplement the principal message (see Comma 4.1).

Examples

Dr. Samuel Goppard's phenomenal prediction (*Business Week*, June 20, 1974) has made some business forecasters revise their techniques.

Smith was elected chairman (the vote was almost 2 to 1), and immediately he introduced his plan for reorganization.

Period

1. The period is primarily used to indicate the end of a declarative sentence. But it does have some other vital uses.

2. After abbreviations or initials, the period is used.

Example

Ph.D., Co., Inc., A.M., A.D., etc.

3. The ellipsis (a series of periods) may be used to indicate the omission of words from a quoted passage. If the omitted part consists of something less than a paragraph, three periods are customarily placed at the point of omission (a fourth period is added if the omission comes at the sentence end). If the omitted part is a paragraph or more, however, a full line of periods is used. In either case the periods are appropriately typed with intervening spaces.

Example

Logical explanations, however, have been given by authorities in the field. Some attribute the decline ... to the changing economy in the state during recent years. ...

. . . .

Added to the labor factor is the high cost of raw material, which has tended to eliminate many marginal producers. Too, the rising cost of electric power in recent years may have shifted many of the industry leader's attention to other forms of production.

Question mark

Sentences which are direct questions are ended with the question mark.

Examples

What are the latest quotations on Ewing-Bell common stock?
Will this campaign help to sell Dunnco products?

Note, however, that the question mark is not used with indirect questions.

Examples

The president was asked whether this campaign will help to sell Dunnco products.

He asked me what the latest quotations on Ewing-Bell common stock were.

Quotation mark

1. Quotation marks are used to enclose the exact words of a speaker or, if the quotation is short, the exact words of a writer.

By short written quotations is meant something four lines or less. Longer quoted passages are best displayed with additional right and left margins (see pages 161-62), in single spacing (where double spacing has been used in the text), and without quotation marks.

Examples

Short written passage: H. G. McVoy sums up his presentation with this statement: "All signs indicate that automation will be evolutionary, not revolutionary."

Verbal quotation: "This really should bring on a production slow-down," said Mr. Kuntz.

If the quoted words are broken by explanation or reference words, each quoted part is enclosed in quotation marks.

Example

"Will you be specific," he asked, "in recommending a course of action?"

2. A quotation within a quotation is indicated by single quotation marks.

Example

President Carver said, "It has been a long time since I have heard an employee say 'boss, I'm going to beat my quota today.'"

3. Periods and commas are always placed inside quotation marks. Semicolons and colons always go outside the marks. Question marks and exclamation points go inside if they apply to the quoted passage and outside if they apply to the whole sentence.

Examples

"If we are patient," he said, "prosperity will some day arrive." [The comma is within the quotes; the period is also within the quotes.]

"Is there a quorum?" he asked. [The question mark belongs to the quoted passage.]

Which of you said, "I know where the error lies"? [The question mark applies to the entire sentence.]

I conclude only this from the union's promise to "force the hand of management": Violence will be their trump card. [Here the colon is not part of the quotation.]

4. Titles of the parts of a publication (articles in a magazine, chapters in a book, etc.) are enclosed in quotation marks. Titles of a whole publication, however, are placed in italics. Italics in typewritten material are indicated by underscoring.

Examples

The third chapter of the book *Elementary Statistical Procedure* is entitled "Concepts of Sampling."

John Glasgow's most recent article, "A Union Boss Views Automation," appears in the current issue of *Fortune*.

Semicolon

1.1. Clauses of a compound sentence that are not joined by a conjunction are separated by a semicolon.

Examples

Cork or asbestos sheeting must be hand-cut; polyurethane may be poured into a mold.

The new contract provides substantial wage increases; the original contract emphasized shorter hours.

Covered by this standard are main clauses connected by conjunctive adverbs. Conjunctive adverbs are really not conjunctions but are such words as *however, nevertheless, therefore, then, moreover, besides*, etc.

Examples

The survey findings indicated a need to revise the policy; nevertheless the president vetoed the amendment.

Small-town buyers favor the old models; therefore the board concluded that both models should be manufactured.

1.2. Standard lists of "weak" connectives of independent clauses include the little words *also, hence, yet,* and *still* and such introductory phrases as *that is, in fact, in other words*, and the like. The test of their weakness as connectives is that, to perform a complete conjunctive function, these words or phrases each need the support of a coordinating conjunction (and *therefore,* and *yet,* and *still,* but *nevertheless,* or *in other words*). With the coordinating conjunctions these forms would take comma punctuation, naturally; but standing alone, they need the semicolon support.

1.3. Note that *so that* introducing a dependent clause of purpose ("They incorporated so that they might limit liability") needs no punctuation mark because its clause is always restrictive.

2. Independent clauses connected by a coordinating conjunction *(and, but, or, for, nor)* may be separated by a semicolon if the clauses are long or have internal punctuation. Sometimes short compound sentences with coordinating conjunctions are separated in order to achieve special emphasis. The purpose of this practice is to help the reader see the break between clauses by not allowing him to be misled by the other punctuation marks.

Examples

The FTU and the IFL, rivals from the beginning of the new industry, have shared almost equally in the growth of membership; but the FTU predominates among workers in the petroleum-products crafts, including pipeline construction and operation, and the IFL leads in memberships of chemical workers.

The market price was $4; but we paid $7.

3. Elements in a series which contains internal commas are separated by semicolons.

Examples

The following gains were made in the February year-to-year comparison: Fort Worth, 7,300; Dallas, 4,705; Lubbock, 2,610; San Antonio, 2,350; Waco, 2,240; Port Arthur, 2,170; and Corpus Christi, 1,420.

Elected for the new term were Amos T. Zelnak, attorney from Cincinnati; Wilbur T. Hoffmeister, stockbroker and president of Hoffmeister Associates of Baltimore; and William P. Peabody, a member of the faculty of the University of Georgia.

4. Use the semicolon between coordinate units only. Do not use it to attach a dependent clause or phrase to an independent clause.

5. Use punctuation marks in consistent echelons of descent—major marks for major units, smaller marks for smaller ones. Do not mix them or reverse them. To use a semicolon, colon, or dash as internal punctuation within a clause or unit already set off by commas is illogical and confusing.

Examples

Not this: His itinerary, which included New York; Portland, Maine; Springfield, Ohio; and Chicago, was revised by the sales manager.

But this: [You'd better recast the whole thing, but this would do.] His itinerary, which included New York, Portland (Maine), Springfield (Ohio), and Chicago, was revised. . . .

Be careful also not to start a parenthetical expression with one mark and end it with another.

STANDARDS FOR CORRECTNESS IN GRAMMAR

As with the review of punctuation standards, the following summary of grammar standards is not intended to be a complete handbook on the subject. Rather, it is a summary of the major trouble spots you are likely to encounter. If you will master them, your chances of miscommunicating will be greatly diminished.

Adjective-adverb confusion

Adjectives should not be used for adverbs, nor should adverbs be used for adjectives. Adjectives modify only nouns and pronouns; and adverbs modify verbs, adjectives, or other adverbs.

Possibly the chief source of this confusion is in statements where the modifier follows the verb. If the modifier refers to the subject, an adjective should be used. If it limits the verb, an adverb is needed.

> *Below standard:* She filed the records *quick.*
> *Acceptable:* She filed the records *quickly.* [Refers to the verb.]
> *Below standard:* John doesn't feel *badly.*
> *Acceptable:* John doesn't feel *bad.* [Refers to the noun.]
> *Below standard:* The new cars look *beautifully.*
> *Acceptable:* The new cars look *beautiful.* [Refers to the noun.]

It should be noted that many words are both adjective and adverb *(little, well, fast, much).* And some adverbs have two forms: One form is the same as the adjective, and the other adds the *ly (slow* and *slowly, cheap* and *cheaply, quick* and *quickly).*

> *Acceptable:* All of our drivers are instructed to drive *slow.*
> *Acceptable:* All of our drivers are instructed to drive *slowly.*

Subject-verb agreement

Nouns and their verbs must agree in number. A plural noun must have a plural verb form; a singular noun must have a singular verb.

Below standard: Expenditures for miscellaneous equipment *was* expected to decline. [*Expenditures* is plural, so its verb must be plural.]

Acceptable: Expenditures for miscellaneous equipment *were* expected to decline.

Below standard: The *president,* as well as his staff, *were* not able to attend. [*President* is the subject, and the number is not changed by the modifying phrase.]

Acceptable: The *president,* as well as his staff, *was* not able to attend.

Compound subjects (two or more nouns joined by *and*) require plural verbs.

Below standard: The *welders and* their *foreman* is in favor of the proposal. [*Welders* and *foreman* are compound subjects of the verb, but *is* is singular.]

Acceptable: The *welders and* their *foreman are* in favor of the proposal.

Below standard: Received in the morning delivery *was a typewriter and* two *reams* of letterhead paper. [*Reams* and *typewriter* are the subjects; the verb must be plural.]

Acceptable: Received in the morning delivery *were* a *typewriter and* two *reams* of letterhead paper.

Collective nouns may be either singular or plural, depending on the meaning intended.

Acceptable: The *committee have* carefully *studied* the proposal. [*Committee* is thought of as separate individuals.]

Acceptable: The *committee has* carefully *studied* the proposal. [The *committee* is considered as a unit.]

As a rule, the pronouns *anybody, anyone, each, either, everyone, everybody, neither, nobody, somebody,* and *someone* take a singular verb. The word *none* may be either singular or plural, depending on whether it is used to refer to a unit or to more than a unit.

Acceptable: Either of the advertising campaigns *is* costly.

Acceptable: Nobody who watches the clock *is successful.*

Adverbial clauses used as noun clauses

Do not use an adverbial clause as a noun clause. Clauses beginning with *because, when, where, if,* and similar adverbial connectives are not properly used as subjects, objects, or complements of verbs.

Not this: He did not know *if* he could go or not.
But this: He did not know *whether* he could go or not.
Not this: The reason was *because* he did not submit a report.
But this: The reason was *that* he did not submit a report.

Not this: A time-series graph is *where* [or *when*] changes in an index such as wholesale prices are indicated.
But this: A time-series graph is the picturing of . . . .

Dangling modifiers

Avoid the use of modifiers which do not logically modify a word in the sentence. Such modifiers are said to dangle. They are both illogical and confusing. Usually, sentences containing dangling constructions can be corrected in either of two ways: The noun or pronoun which the modifier describes may be inserted, or the dangling element may be changed to a complete clause.

Below standard: Believing that credit customers should have advance notice of the sale, special letters were mailed to them.
Acceptable: Believing that credit customers should have advance notice of the sale, we mailed special letters to them. [Improvement is made by inserting the pronoun modified.]
Acceptable: Because we believed that credit customers should have advance notice of the sale, we mailed special letters to them. [Improvement is made by changing the dangling element to a complete clause.]

Dangling modifiers are of four principal types: participial phrases, elliptical clauses, gerund phrases, and infinitive phrases.

Below standard: Believing that District 7 was not being thoroughly covered, an additional salesman was assigned to the area. [Dangling participial phrase.]
Acceptable: Believing that District 7 was not being thoroughly covered, the sales manager assigned an additional salesman to the area.
Below standard: After hearing his convincing arguments, my vote was changed. [Dangling gerund phrase.]
Acceptable: After hearing his convincing arguments, I changed my vote.
Below standard: To succeed at this job, long hours and hard work must not be shunned. [Dangling infinitive phrase.]
Acceptable: To succeed at this job, one must not shun long hours and hard work.

Below standard: While waiting on a customer, the radio was stolen. [Dangling elliptical clause—a clause without noun or verb.]

Acceptable: While the salesman was waiting on a customer, the radio was stolen.

There are, however, a few generally accepted introductory phrases which are permitted to dangle. Included in this group are *generally speaking, confidentially speaking, taking all things into consideration,* and such expressions as *in boxing, in welding,* and *in farming.*

Acceptable: Generally speaking, business activity is at an all time high.

Acceptable: In farming, the land must be prepared long before planting time.

Acceptable: Taking all things into consideration, this applicant is the best for the job.

The sentence fragment

The sentence fragment should be avoided. Although it may sometimes be used for effect, as in sales writing, it is best omitted by all but the most skilled writers. The sentence fragment consists of any group of words which cannot stand up alone as a complete and independent statement. Probably the most frequent violation of this rule results from the use of a subordinate clause as a sentence.

Below standard: Believing that you will want an analysis of sales for November. We have sent you the figures.

Acceptable: Believing that you will want an analysis of sales for November, we have sent you the figures.

Below standard: He declared that such a procedure would not be practical. And that it would be too expensive in the long run.

Acceptable: He declared that such a procedure would not be practical and that it would be too expensive in the long run.

Parallelism

1. Parts of a sentence that are used to express parallel thoughts should be parallel in grammatical form. Parallel constructions are logically connected by the coordinating conjunctions *and, but,* and *or.* Care should be taken to see that the sentence elements connected by these conjunctions are of the same grammatical type. That is, if

one of the parts is a noun, so should the other parts be nouns. If one of the parts is an infinitive phrase, so should the other parts be infinitive phrases.

> *Below standard:* The company objectives for the coming year are to match last year's production, higher sales, and improving consumer relations.
> *Acceptable:* The company objectives for the coming year are to match last year's production, to increase sales, and to improve consumer relations.
> *Below standard:* Writing copy may be more valuable experience than to make layouts.
> *Acceptable:* Writing copy may be more valuable experience than making layouts.
> *Below standard:* The questionnaire asks for this information: number of employees, what is our union status, and how much do we pay.
> *Acceptable:* The questionnaire asks for this information: number of employees, union affiliation, and pay scale.

2. After each member of a correlating pair of conjunctions *(either, or; both, and; not only, but also)*, use exactly the same grammatical form.

3. Comparisons in particular need to be kept on consistent bases. Do not fall into the ditch of jargonese shortcuts.

4. Avoid the faulty parallelism of the illogical *and which* construction. Do not tie a lone relative clause to the main clause with *and*, as if it were parallel with a minor adjective, participial modifier, or implied quality.

> He warned of the high and frightening cost-of-living index, and which is still rising.
> *Better:* He warned of the cost-of-living index, which is frighteningly high and which is still rising.
> *Or:* He warned that the frightening high cost-of-living index is still rising.

Pronouns

1. The antecedents of all pronouns should be unmistakably clear. Failure to conform to this standard causes confusion. Confusion is likely to come about particularly in sentences where two or more nouns are possible antecedents of the pronoun or where the antecedent is far removed from the pronoun.

Below standard: When the president objected to Mr. Carter, he told him to mind his own business. [Who told whom?]

Acceptable: When the president objected to Mr. Carter, Mr. Carter told him to mind his own business.

Below standard: The mixture should not be allowed to boil; so when you do it, watch the temperature gauge. [*It* doesn't have an antecedent.]

Acceptable: The mixture should not be allowed to boil; so when conducting the experiment, watch the temperature gauge.

Below standard: The model V is being introduced this year. Ads in *Time, Business Week,* and big-city newspapers over the country are designed to get sales off to a good start. It is especially designed for the novice boatman who is not willing to pay a big price.

Acceptable: The model V is being introduced this year. Ads in *Time, Business Week,* and big-city newspapers over the country are designed to get sales off to a good start. The new model is especially designed for the novice boatman who is not willing to pay a big price.

Confusion may sometimes result from using a pronoun with an implied antecedent.

Below standard: Because of the disastrous freeze in the citrus belt, it was necessary that most of them be replanted.

Acceptable: Because of the disastrous freeze in the citrus belt, it is necessary that most of the citrus orchards be replanted.

Except when their reference is perfectly clear, it is best to avoid using the pronouns *which, that,* and *this* to refer to a whole idea of a preceding clause. Many times the sentence can be made clear by the use of a clarifying noun following the pronoun.

Below standard (following a detailed presentation of the writer's suggestion for improving a company's suggestion-box plan): This should be put into effect without delay.

Acceptable: This suggestion-box plan should be put into effect right away.

2. The number of the pronoun should agree with the number of its antecedent. If the antecedent is singular, its pronoun must be singular. If the antecedent is plural, its pronoun must be plural.

Below standard: Taxes and insurance are necessary evils in any business, and it must be considered carefully in anticipating profits.

Acceptable: Taxes and insurance are necessary evils in any business, and they must be considered carefully in anticipating profits.

108

Below standard: Everybody should make plans for their retirement. [Words like *everyone, everybody, anybody* are singular.]
Acceptable: Everybody should make plans for his retirement.

3. Care should be taken to use the correct case of the pronoun. If the pronoun serves as the subject of the verb, or if it follows a form of the infinitive *to be,* a nominative case pronoun should be used. (Nominative case of the personal pronouns is *I, you, he, she, it, we, they.*)

Acceptable: He will record the minutes of the meeting.
Acceptable: I think it will be he.

If the pronoun is the object of a preposition or a verb, or if it is the subject of an infinitive, the objective case should be used. (Objective case for the personal pronouns is *me, you, him, her, us, them.*)

Below standard: This transaction is between you and *he.* [*He* is nominative and cannot be the object of the preposition *between.*]
Acceptable: This transaction is between you and *him.*
Below standard: Because the investigator praised Mr. Smith and *I,* we were promoted.
Acceptable: Because the investigator praised Mr. Smith and *me,* we were promoted.

The case of relative pronouns *(who, whom)* is determined by the pronoun's use in the clause it introduces. One good way of determining which case should be used is to substitute the personal pronoun for the relative pronoun. If the case of the personal pronoun which fits is nominative, *who* should be used. If it is objective, *whom* should be used.

Acceptable: George Cutler is the salesman who won the award. [*He* (nominative) could be substituted for the relative pronoun; therefore, nominative *who* should be used.]
Acceptable: George Cutler is the salesman *whom* you recommended. [Objective-case *him* would substitute. Thus, objective-case *whom* is used.]

Usually the possessive case is used with substantives which immediately precede a gerund (verbal noun ending in *ing*).

Acceptable: Our selling of the stock frightened some of the conservative members of the board.
Acceptable: His accepting the money ended his legal claim to the property.

Tense

The tense of each verb, infinitive, and participle used should reflect the logical time of happening of the statement: Every statement has its place in time. If this place in time is to be exactly communicated, the writer must take care of his selection of tense. Even though tense usually is determined by the subject of the statement being reported, a few trouble spots may be mentioned.

1. *Statements of fact that are true at the time of writing should be worded in the present tense.*

Below standard: Boston was not selected as a site for the aircraft plant because it *was* too near the coast. [Boston still is near the coast, isn't it?]

Acceptable: Boston was not selected as a site for the aircraft plant because it *is* too near the coast.

2. Past tense is used in statements covering a definite past event or action.

Acceptable: Mr. Burns *said* to me, "Bill, you'll never make an auditor."

Below standard: Mr. Burns *says* to me, "Bill, you'll never make an auditor."

3. The time period reflected by the past participle (*having been* . . .) is earlier than that of its governing verb. For the present participle (*being* . . .), the time period reflected is the same as that of the governing verb.

Below standard: These debentures are among the oldest on record, *being* issued in early 1937.

Acceptable: These debentures are among the oldest on record, *having been* issued in early 1937.

Below standard: Mr. Sloan, *having been* the top salesman on the force, was made sales manager. [Possible but illogical.]

Acceptable: Mr. Sloan, *being* the top salesman on the force, was made sales manager.

4. Verbs in subordinate clauses are governed by the verb in the principal clause. When the main verb is in the past tense, usually the subordinate verb must also be in a past tense (past, present perfect, or past perfect). Thus, if the time of the subordinate clause is the same as that of the main verb, past tense is used.

Acceptable: I *noticed* [past tense] the discrepancy, and then I *remembered* [same time as main verb] the incidents which caused it.

If the time of the subordinate clause is previous to that of the main verb in past tense, past perfect tense is used for the subordinate verb.

Below standard: In early July we *noticed* [past] that he *exceeded* [logically should be previous to main verb] his quota three times.

Acceptable: In early July we *noticed* that he *had exceeded* his quota three times.

The present perfect tense is used for the subordinate clause when the time of this clause is subsequent to the time of the main verb.

Below standard: Before the war we *contributed* [past] generously, but lately we *forget* [should be time subsequent to the time of main verb] our duties.

Acceptable: Before the war we *contributed* generously, but lately we *have forgotten* our duties.

5. The present perfect tense does not logically refer to a definite time in the past. Instead, it indicates time somewhere in the indefinite past.

Below standard: We *have audited* your records on July 31 of 1973 and 1974.

Acceptable: We *audited* your records on July 31 of 1973 and 1974.

Acceptable: We *have audited* your records twice in the past.

Word use

Misused words call attention to themselves and detract from the writing. Although the possibilities of error in word use are infinite, the following list contains a few of the most common ones.

Don't use	*Use*
a long ways	a long way
and etc.	etc.
anywheres	anywhere
different than	different from
have got to	must
in back of	behind
in hopes of	in hope of
in regards to	in regard to
inside of	within
kind of satisfied	somewhat satisfied
nowhere near	not nearly

Don't use	*Use*
nowheres	nowhere
off of	off
over with	over
seldom ever	seldom
try and come	try to come

STANDARDS FOR THE USE OF NUMBERS

Often, many of the reports you write are to some extent quantitative. Thus, knowing when you should spell out a number and when you should present it in its numeral form is likely to be a problem. As with other matters of correctness, authorities do not all agree on matters of number usage. In view of this confusion, the following standards are those we believe to be most practical and most widely accepted.

Numbers

1. Although authorities do not agree on number usage, the business writer would do well to follow the rule of ten. By this rule, one spells out number ten and below. He uses figures for numbers above ten.

> *Correct:* The auditor found 13 discrepancies in the stock records.
> *Correct:* The auditor found nine discrepancies in the stock records.

As with most rules, this one has exceptions.

2. An exception to the rule of ten is made when a number begins a sentence. In this position the number is spelled out regardless of size.

> *Correct:* Seventy-three bonds were destroyed.
> *Correct:* Eighty-nine men picketed the north entrance.

3. In comparisons it is best to keep all numbers in the same form. The form used should be the one that according to the rule of ten, would be used most often in the series.

> *Correct:* We managed to salvage three lathes, one drill, and thirteen welding machines.
> *Correct:* Sales increases over last year were 9 percent on automotive parts, 14 percent on hardware, and 23 percent on appliances.

4. When two series of numbers appear in one sentence, one should be spelled out, and the other should be in numeral form.

Correct: Three salesmen exceeded $1,500, fourteen exceeded $1,000, and thirty-one exceeded $500.

5. Days of the month are typed in figure form when they are preceded by the month.

Correct: July 3, 1971

When they appear alone, or when they precede the month, the days of the month may be either spelled out or in numeral form according to the rule of ten.

Correct: I shall be there on the 13th.
Correct: The union scheduled the strike vote for the eighth.
Correct: Mr. Millican signed the contract on the seventh of July.
Correct: Sales have declined since the 14th of August.

7

Use of graphic aids

Because your reports frequently must communicate complex and voluminous information, you are likely to have difficulty making words do the job. In a statistical analysis, for example, you are likely to get your reader lost in a maze of data as you tell the report's story in words. Or in a technical report you are likely to find difficulty attempting to use words to describe a process or a procedure. Frequently, in such cases you will need to use pictures of one kind or other to help communicate your information.

SELECTION AND USE

Pictures, or "graphic aids," as we call them in report writing, are an essential part of many reports. Rarely do they take the place of words, for words are essential for communicating the information in most reports. Their role is more a supplementary one—one of assisting the words to communicate the report content. In addition to this communication role, graphic aids also serve to present minor supporting details not covered in words. They help to give emphasis to the key points of coverage. Also, they serve to improve the physical appearance of the report, thereby making it more inviting and readable.

Foresight in planning

If you are to use graphic aids effectively, you must plan them with foresight and care. Such planning is a part of the task of organizing the report.

As you approach the task of planning your graphic aids, you should keep in mind your fundamental purpose of communicating. Thus, you should never arbitrarily select some random number of illustrations to include. Nor should you judge the completeness of graphic presentation in a report by the number of illustrations used. Instead, you should plan each graphic aid for a specific communication reason. Each one should help to present your report information. Each one should be included because it is needed.

Relationship of need to the plan

Just what graphic aids you will need to communicate a report's story, however, is not easy to determine. Much depends on your overall plan. If you plan to cover the subject in detail, the role of the graphic aids is to emphasize and to supplement. Specifically, they point up the major facts discussed and present the detailed data not covered in the writing. On the other hand, if you plan to present the facts in summary form, you may use the graphic aids to work more closely with your text.

The first of these arrangements (complete text supplemented by graphic aids) is conventional and is best for all studies when completeness is a main requirement. The second plan (summary text closely helped by graphic aids) is gaining in importance. It is especially used in popular types of reports, such as those addressed to the general public. As illustrated in Figure 7-1, this plan produces fast-moving, light reading—the kind the public likes. In addition to the public, many top executives prefer this plan. With the increasing demands on their time, these executives prefer that the reports they read give them the facts quickly and easily. Short, summary reports, helped by an abundance of clear graphic aids, do this job best. Frequently, because of the need for a complete report for future reference and the need for presentation of summary information to the top executives, both kinds of reports are written for the same problem.

FIGURE 7-1
Page from a popular report illustrating use of a summary text closely helped by graphic aids

Long Industry Lead Times

In considering measures to ease the energy supply situation (section VI), the importance of long lead times cannot be overemphasized. In some activities a sufficient concentration of brains and money can solve problems through "crash" action. In the oil industry, however, as the diagram below shows, planners must think in terms of several years, not months. An understanding of the time factor in oil operations is fundamental.

CHART 15

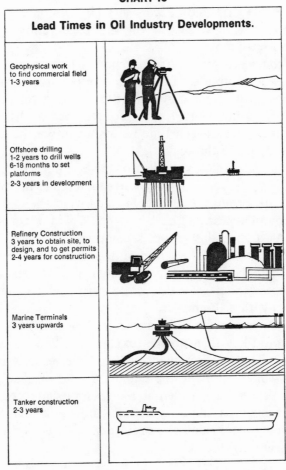

Lead Times in Oil Industry Developments.

Geophysical work
to find commercial field
1-3 years

Offshore drilling
1-2 years to drill wells
6-18 months to set
platforms
2-3 years in development

Refinery Construction
3 years to obtain site, to
design, and to get permits
2-4 years for construction

Marine Terminals
3 years upwards

Tanker construction
2-3 years

Preferred placement within the report

For the maximum communication effect, you should place the graphic aids which help tell the report story within the report and near the text they will illustrate. In such positions, they are likely to be seen at the time they need to be seen.

Exactly where you should place each illustration is determined by its size. If the graphic aid is small, taking up only a portion of the page, you should place it so that it is surrounded by the writing covering it. If the graphic aid requires a full page for display, you should place it immediately following the page on which it is discussed. When the discussion covers several pages, however, the full-page illustration is best placed on the page following the first reference to its content.

There is some acceptance of the report arrangement in which all of the illustrations are placed in the appendix. Aside from the time saved by the typist, there is little that can be said for this practice. Certainly, it does not work for the convenience of the reader who must flip through pages each time he wishes to see the graphic presentation of a part of the text.

The graphic aids which you wish to include but which do not tell a specific part of the report's story you should place in the appendix. Included in this group are all graphic aids which belong within the report for completeness, yet have no specific spot of coverage within the study. As a rule, this group is comprised of long and complex tables which may cover large areas of information. These tables may even cover the data displayed in a number of charts and other more graphic devices which generally are constructed to illustrate very specific spots within the report.

Whether you place the illustrations within or at the end of the text, you should key them to the text portion they cover by means of references. That is, you might well call the reader's attention to illustrations which cover the topic under discussion. Such references you can make best as incidental remarks in sentences containing significant comments about the data shown in the illustration. Although numerous incidental wordings may be used, the following word groups are acceptable:

..., as shown in Chart 4....
.., indicated in Chart 4....
.., as a glance at Chart 4 reveals....
...(see Chart 4)....

MECHANICS OF CONSTRUCTION

In planning the illustrations, and later in the actual work of constructing them, you will be confronted with numerous questions of mechanics. Many of these questions must be solved through intelligent appraisal of the conditions concerned in each instance. But the mechanics fall into general groups, the most conventional of which are summarized in the following paragraphs.

Size determination

One of the first decisions involved in constructing a graphic aid is that of determining how large it should be. The answer to this question should not be arbitrary, nor should it be based solely on your convenience. Instead, you should seek to give the illustration the size that its contents justify. If, for example, an illustration is relatively simple, comprising only two or three quantities, a quarter page might be adequate. Certainly, a full page would not be needed to illustrate the data. But if a graphic aid is made up of a dozen or so quantities, more space would be justified—possibly even a full page.

With extremely complex and involved data, it may be necessary to make the graphic aid larger than the report page. Such long presentations must be carefully inserted and folded within the report so that they open easily. The fold selected will of course vary with the size of the page, so there is no best fold that can be recommended. You would do well to survey whatever possibilities are available to you.

Layout arrangement

The layout of any graphic aid is influenced by the amount of information being illustrated. But whenever it is practical, it is best to keep the layout of the illustration within the normal page layout.

Rules and borders

You should arrange rules and borders of any form of graphic presentation to help display and to make clear the data presented. Thus, you should determine their use chiefly through careful planning. As a general practice, however, you should set off graphic aids of less than a page from the text by a lined border which completely encloses the illustration and its caption. You may use this arrangement for full-page illustrations as well, although with such pages the border does not serve so practical a purpose. You should not extend the borders beyond the normal page margins. An exception to this rule is, of course, the unusual instance in which the volume of data to be illustrated simply will not fit into an area less than the normal page layout.

Color and cross-hatching

Color and/or cross-hatching appropriately used, helps the reader to see the comparisons and distinctions. In addition, they give the report a boost in physical attractiveness. Color is especially valuable for this purpose, and you should use it whenever practical.

Numbering

Except for minor tabular displays which are actually a part of the text, you should number all illustrations in the report. Many schemes of numbering are available to you, depending on the makeup of the graphic aids.

If you have many graphic aids which fall into two or more categories, each category may be numbered consecutively. For example, if your report is illustrated by six tables, five charts, and six maps, these graphic aids may be numbered Table 1, Table 2, . . . Table 6; Chart 1, Chart 2, . . . Chart 5; and Map 1, Map 2, . . . Map 6.

But if the illustrations used are a wide mixture of types, you may number them in two groups: tables and figures. To illustrate, consider a report containing three tables, two maps, three charts, one diagram, and one photograph. These graphic aids could be grouped and numbered as Table I, Table II, and Table III, and Figure 1, Figure 2, . . . Figure 7. By convention, tables are never grouped with other forms of presentation. *Figures* represent a sort of miscellaneous grouping which may include all illustration types other than tables. It would not be wrong to group and number as figures all graphic aids other than tables even if the group contained sufficient subgroups (charts, maps, etc.) to warrant separate numbering of each of these subgroups.

As the preceding examples illustrate, tables are conventionally numbered with capital roman numerals (I, II, III, etc.). All other forms of illustration use the arabic numerals (1, 2, 3, etc.). There is some tendency nowadays, however, to use arabic numerals for all forms. Obviously, the most important rule to follow in regard to numbering is that of consistency.

Construction of title captions

Every graphic aid should have a title caption which adequately describes the contents. Like the captions used in other parts of the report, the title to the graphic aid has the objective of concisely covering the illustration contents. As a check of content coverage, you might well use the journalist's five W's—*who, what, where, when, why.* Sometimes you might include *how* (the classification principle). But as conciseness of expression is also desired, it is not always necessary to include all of the W's in the caption constructed. A title of a chart comparing annual sales volume of Texas and Louisiana stores of the Brill Company for the 1974-19— period might be constructed as follows:

Who: Brill Company
What: Annual sales
Where: Texas and Louisiana
When: 1974-19—
Why: For comparison

The caption might read, "Comparative annual sales of Texas and Louisiana branches of the Brill Company, 1974-19—."

Placement of titles

Titles of tables are conventionally placed above the tabular display. Titles to all other graphic presentations usually are placed below the illustration. There is convention, too, for placing table titles in a higher type (usually solid capitals without the underscore in typewritten reports) than titles of all other illustrations. But nowadays these conventional forms are not universally followed. There is a growing tendency to use lowercase type for all illustration titles and to place titles of both tables and charts at the top. These more recent practices are simple and logical; yet for formal reports you should follow the conventional arrangement.

Footnotes and acknowledgments

Occasionally, parts of a graphic aid require special explanation or elaboration. When these conditions come up, just as when similar explanations are made within the text of the report, you should use footnotes. Such footnotes are nothing more than concise explanations placed below the illustration and keyed to the part explained by means of a superscript (raised number) or asterisk, as shown in Figure 7-2. Footnotes for tables are best placed immediately below the graphic presentation. Footnotes for other graphic forms follow the illustration when the title is placed at the bottom of the page.

FIGURE 7-2
Good arrangement of the parts of a typical table

TABLE NO. TITLE OF TABLE				
Stub head	CAPTION HEAD			
	Subcaption	Subcaption	Subcaption	Subcaption
Stub	X X X	X X X	X X X	X X X
Stub	X X X	X X X	X X X	X X X
Stub	X X X	X X X	X X X	X X X
Stub	X X X	X X X	X X X	X X X
"	"	"	"	"
"	"	"	"	"
"	"	"	"	"
"	"	"	"	"
"	"	"	"	"
"	"	"	"	"
TOTAL	X X X	X X X	X X X	X X X
Footnotes				
Source note:				

Usually, a source acknowledgment is the bottom entry made on the page. By source acknowledgment is meant a reference to the body or authority which deserves the credit for gathering the data used in the illustration. The entry consists simply of the word *source* followed by a colon and the source name. A source note for data based on information gathered by the United States Department of Agriculture might read like this:

Source: United States Department of Agriculture.

If the data were collected by you or your staff, two procedures may be followed. You may give the source as "primary," in which case the source note would read:

Source: Primary.

Or you may omit the source note.

CONSTRUCTION OF TABLES

A table is any systematic arrangement of quantitative information in rows and columns. Although tables are not truly graphic in the literal meaning of the word, they are instrumental in communicating information. Therefore, you may appropriately consider them a part of the graphic-aids planning of your report. The purpose of a table is to present a broad area of information in convenient and orderly fashion. By such an arrangement, the information is simplified, and comparisons and analyses are made easy.

Two basic types of tables are available to you—the general-purpose table and the special-purpose table. General-purpose tables are arrangements of a broad area of data collected. They are repositories of detailed statistical data and have no special analytical purpose. As a rule, general-purpose tables are placed in the report appendix.

Special-purpose tables, as their name implies, are prepared for a special purpose—to help to illustrate a particular phase of the text. Usually, they consist of data carefully drawn from the general-purpose tables. Only those data are selected which are pertinent to the analysis, and sometimes these data are rearranged or regrouped to better illustrate their special purpose. Such tables belong within the text near the spot they illustrate.

Aside from the title, footnotes, and source designation previously discussed, the table consists of stubs, captions, and columns and rows of data, as shown in Figure 7-2. Stubs are the titles to the rows of data, and captions are the titles to the columns. The captions, however, may be divided into subcaptions—or column heads, as they are sometimes called.

As you should plan the text tables specifically, their construction is largely influenced by their illustration purpose. Nevertheless, a few general rules may be listed:

1. If rows tend to be long, repeat the stubs at the right.
2. Use the dash or the abbreviation *n.a.,* but not the zero, to indicate that data are not available.
3. Key the footnote references to numbers in the table with asterisks, daggers, double daggers, etc. Numbers followed by footnote reference numbers might cause confusion.
4. Make totals and subtotals whenever they help the purpose of the table. You may include totals for each column and sometimes for each row. Usually, you will make row totals, but when you desire to give emphasis to the totals, you may place them at the left. Likewise, you should include column totals at the bottom, but you may place them at the top of the column when you want to emphasize these totals. You should separate the totals from their data by a ruled line, usually a double one.
5. Make clear the units in which you record the data. Unit descriptions (bushels, acres, pounds, and the like) are appropriately placed above the columns as part of the captions or subcaptions. If the data are in dollars, however, you should place the dollar mark ($) before the first entry in each column.

THE SIMPLE BAR CHART

Simple bar charts are graphic means of comparing simple magnitudes by the lengths of equal-width bars. You should use such charts to show quantity changes over time, quantity changes over geographic distance, or quantitative distances.

The principal parts of the bar chart are the bars and the grid. The bars may be arranged horizontally or perpendicularly, and each has in its beginning a title identifying the quantity being illustrated. The grid upon which the bars are placed is simply a field carefully ruled by line marks arithmetically scaled to the magnitudes illustrated. Usually, a finely marked grid is made as a preliminary step in constructing a bar chart, and the bars are then placed on the grid. But the final drawing of the chart is best made to show only sufficient grid lines to help the reader's eye measure the magnitudes of the bars. These scaled grid lines are carefully labeled with numerals, and the unit in which the values are measured is indicated by a scale caption appearing below the values in a vertical bar chart and above the values in a horizontal bar arrangement.

Although there are numerous acceptable variations in bar-chart construction, a basic pattern should be helpful to you. Such a pattern, as illustrated in Figure 7-3, is generally adequate.

FIGURE 7-3
Illustration of good arrangement of the parts of a simple bar chart.

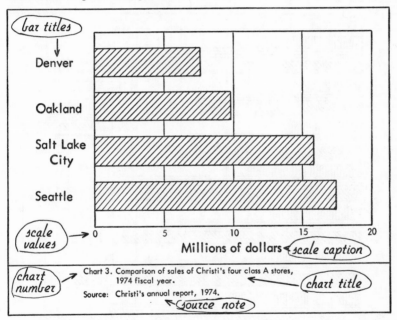

VARIATIONS OF THE BAR CHART

In addition to the simple bar chart just described, you may use a number of other types of bar charts in presenting a report. The more commonly used of these variants are the multiple bar chart, the bilateral bar chart, and the subdivided or component-part bar chart.

Multiple bar charts

Comparisons of two or three variables within a single bar chart are made possible by the use of multiple bars distinguished by cross-hatching, shading, or color. That is, the bars representing each of the variables being compared are distinguished by these mechanical means, as illustrated in Figure 7-4. The key to the variables is given in a legend, which may be placed within the illustration or below it, depending on where space is available. Generally, it is confusing and therefore inadvisable to make multiple comparisons of this type when more than three variables are involved.

FIGURE 7-4
Multiple bar chart

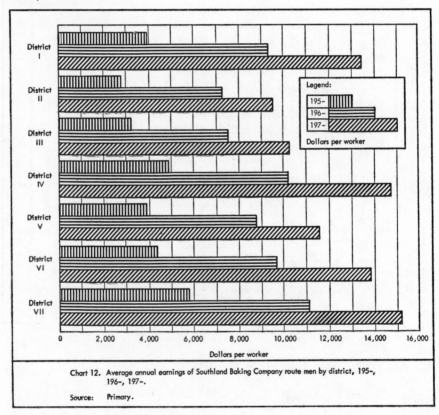

Chart 12. Average annual earnings of Southland Baking Company route men by district, 195-, 196-, 197-.

Source: Primary.

Bilateral bar charts

When it is necessary to show plus or minus deviations, you may use bilateral bar charts. The bars of these charts begin at a central point of reference and may go either up or down, as illustrated in Figure 7-5. Bar titles may be written either within, above, or below the bars, depending on which placement best fits the illustration. Bilateral bar charts are especially good for showing percentage change, but you may use them for any series in which minus quantities are present.

FIGURE 7-5
Bilateral bar chart

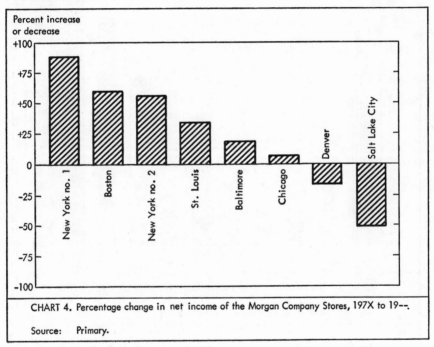

CHART 4. Percentage change in net income of the Morgan Company Stores, 197X to 19--.

Source: Primary.

Subdivided bar charts

If it is desirable for you to show the composition of magnitudes being compared, you may use subdivided bar charts. In this form of chart, cross-hatchings, shadings, or colors are first assigned to each of the parts to be shown; then the bars are marked off into their component parts, as Figure 7-6 illustrates. As in all cases where cross-hatching or color is used, a legend is employed to guide the reader.

FIGURE 7-6
Illustration of a subdivided bar chart

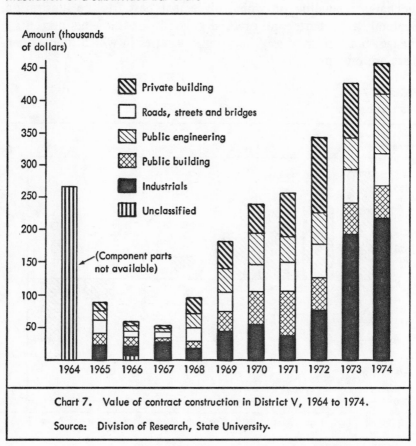

Chart 7. Value of contract construction in District V, 1964 to 1974.

Source: Division of Research, State University.

A form of the subdivided bar chart frequently is used to compare the composition of variables by percentages. This chart differs from the typical bar chart principally in that the bar lengths are meaningless in the comparisons. All the bars are of equal length, and only the component parts of the bars vary. As depicted in Figure 7-7, the component parts may be labeled, but they may also be explained in a legend.

FIGURE 7-7
Illustration of a subdivided bar chart

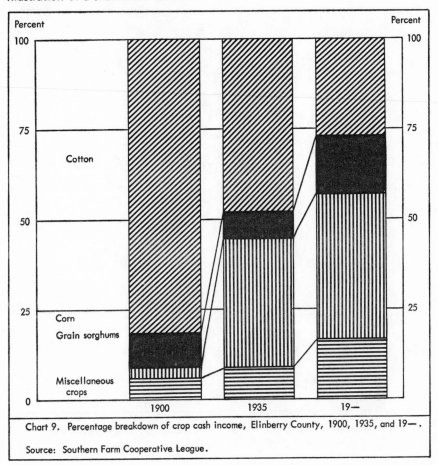

Chart 9. Percentage breakdown of crop cash income, Elinberry County, 1900, 1935, and 19—.

Source: Southern Farm Cooperative League.

Pictograms

A pictogram is a bar chart which uses pertinent pictures rather than bars to put over the information. For example, a company seeking to show graphically its profits from sales could use a simple bar chart for the purpose. Or the firm could use instead of bars a line of coins equal in length to the bars. Coins might be selected because they depict the information to be illustrated. This resulting graphic form, as illustrated in Figure 7-8, is the pictogram.

In general, construction of pictograms follows the procedure used

FIGURE 7-8
Illustration of the pictogram

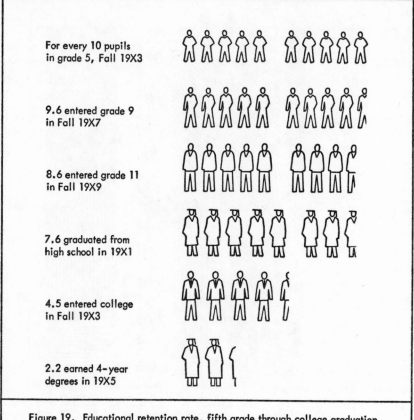

For every 10 pupils
in grade 5, Fall 19X3

9.6 entered grade 9
in Fall 19X7

8.6 entered grade 11
in Fall 19X9

7.6 graduated from
high school in 19X1

4.5 entered college
in Fall 19X3

2.2 earned 4-year
degrees in 19X5

Figure 19. Educational retention rate, fifth grade through college graduation,
United States, 19X3 to 19X5.

Source: U.S. Department of Health, Education, and Welfare.

in constructing bar charts. But two special rules should be followed. First, all of the picture units used must be of equal size. The comparisons must be made wholly on the basis of the number of illustrations used and never by varying the areas of the individual pictures. The reason for this rule is obvious. The human eye is grossly inadequate in comparing areas of geometric designs. Second, the pictures or symbols used must appropriately depict the quantity to be illustrated. A comparison of the navies of the world, for example, might make use of miniature ship drawings. Cotton production might be shown by bales of cotton. Obviously, the drawings used must be immediately interpreted by the reader.

PIE CHART CONSTRUCTION

Also of primary importance in comparing the percentage composition of variables is the pie chart (Figure 7-9). As the name implies, the pie chart illustrates the magnitude being studied as a pie, and the component parts of this whole are shown as slices of this pie. The slices may be individually labeled, or cross-hatching or coloring with an explanatory legend may be used. As it is difficult to judge the

FIGURE 7-9
Illustration of a pie chart

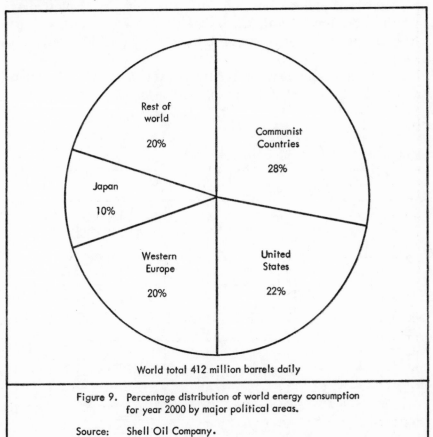

Figure 9. Percentage distribution of world energy consumption for year 2000 by major political areas.

Source: Shell Oil Company.

value of each slice with the naked eye, it is advisable to include the units of value within each slice. A good rule to follow is to begin slicing the pie at the 12 o'clock position and to move around clockwise. It is usually best to show the slices in descending order of magnitude.

You should never use pie diagrams to show comparisons of two or more wholes by means of varying the areas of wholes. Such comparisons are almost meaningless. The human eye is totally inadequate to judge the relative areas of most geometric shapes.

ARRANGEMENT OF THE LINE CHART

Line charts are best used to show the movements or changes of a continuous series of data over time, such as changes in prices, weekly sales totals, and periodic employment data. They may be plotted on an arithmetic, semilogarithmic, or logarithmic grid; but since the arithmetic plot is most common to business reports, it is described here.

In a line chart the item to be illustrated is plotted as a continuous line on a grid. On the grid, time is plotted on the horizontal axis

FIGURE 7-10

Example of a line chart with one series

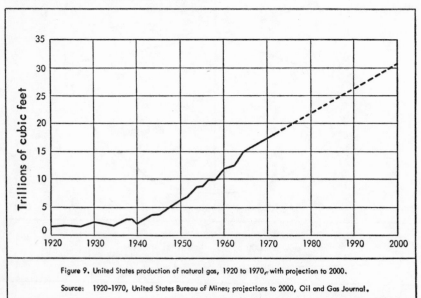

Figure 9. United States production of natural gas, 1920 to 1970, with projection to 2000.

Source: 1920-1970, United States Bureau of Mines; projections to 2000, Oil and Gas Journal.

(*X*-axis); the values of the series are plotted on the vertical axis (*Y*-axis). The scale values and time periods are clearly marked on the axis lines, as shown in Figure 7-10.

Comparisons of two or more series (Figure 7-11) on the same

FIGURE 7-11
Illustration of a line chart comparing more than one series

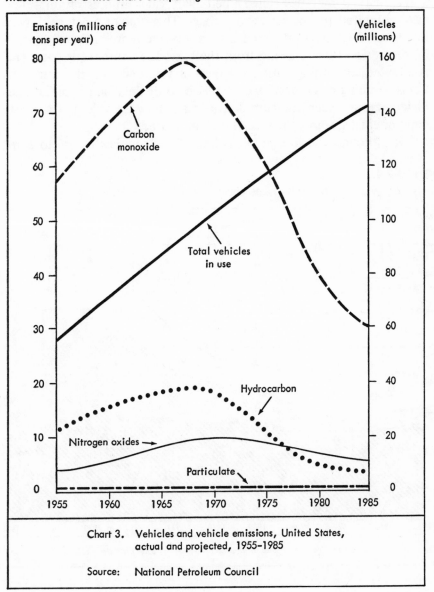

Chart 3.   Vehicles and vehicle emissions, United States, actual and projected, 1955–1985

Source: National Petroleum Council

grid may also be made on a line chart. In such a comparison the lines should be clearly distinguished by color or form (dots, dashes, dots and dashes, and the like) and should be clearly labeled or explained by a legend somewhere in the chart. But the number of series that may be compared on a single grid is limited. As a practical rule, four or five series on a single grid should be a maximum.

It is possible, also, to show component parts of a series by use of a line chart—sometimes called a belt chart. Such an illustration, however, is limited to one series to a chart. This type of chart, as shown in Figure 7-12, is constructed with a top line representing the total of the series; then, starting from the base, the component parts are cumulated, beginning with the largest and ending with the smallest. Cross-hatching or coloring may be used to distinguish the parts. The differences between the cumulative totals show the values of the last component part brought into the cumulation.

Even though the line graph is one of the simplest charts to con-

FIGURE 7-12

Illustration of a component-part line chart

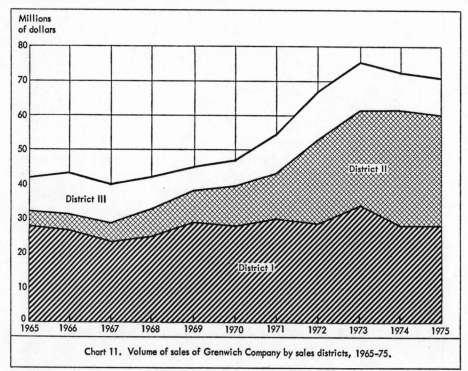

Chart 11. Volume of sales of Grenwich Company by sales districts, 1965–75.

struct, three common pitfalls should be warned against. First of these is the common violation of the rule of zero origin. The Y-scale (vertical axis) must begin at zero even though the points to be plotted are relatively high in value. If most of the points to be plotted are relatively high in value, the comparison may be facilitated by breaking the scale somewhere between zero and the level of the lowest plotted value. Of the numerous means of showing scale these two techniques are recommended:

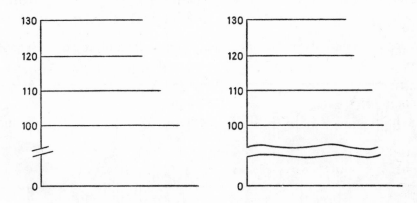

Second, equal magnitudes on both X- and Y-scales should be represented on the grid by equal distances. Any deviation from this rule would distort the illustration, thereby deceiving the reader.

A third common violation of good line-chart construction concerns the determination of proportions on the grid. It is easy to see that by expanding one scale and contracting the other, impressions of extreme deviation can be made. For example, data plotted on a line chart with time intervals one sixteenth of an inch apart certainly appear to show more violent fluctuations than the same data plotted on a chart with time intervals plotted a half inch apart. Only the application of common sense can prevent this violation. The grid distances selected simply must be such as will tend to make the presentation of the data realistic.

DESIGN OF THE STATISTICAL MAP

Maps may also be used to help communicate quantitative information. They are primarily useful when quantitative information is to be compared by geographic areas. On such maps the geographic areas are clearly outlined, and the differences between areas are shown by some graphic technique. Of the numerous techniques that may be used, four are most common.

1. Possibly the most popular technique is that showing quantitative differences of areas by color, shading, or cross-hatching (Figure 7-13). Such maps, of course, must have a legend to explain the quantitative meanings of the various colors, cross-hatchings, and so forth.

FIGURE 7-13

Illustration of a statistical map showing quantitative differences of areas by cross-hatching

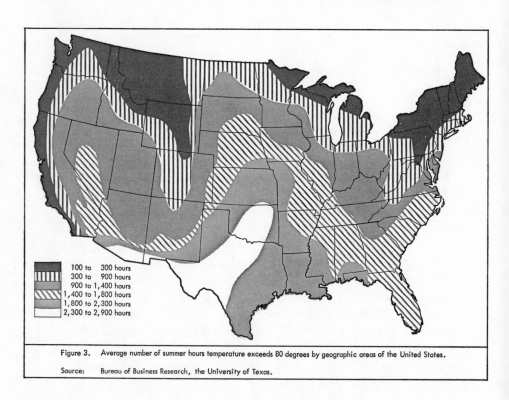

Figure 3. Average number of summer hours temperature exceeds 80 degrees by geographic areas of the United States.

Source: Bureau of Business Research, the University of Texas.

2. Placing the quantities in numerical form within each geographic area, as shown in Figure 7-14, is another widely used technique.
3. Dots, each representing a definite quantity (Figure 7-15), may be placed within the geographic areas in proportion to the quantities to be illustrated for each area.

FIGURE 7-14

Statistical map showing quantitative differences by means of numbers placed within geographic areas

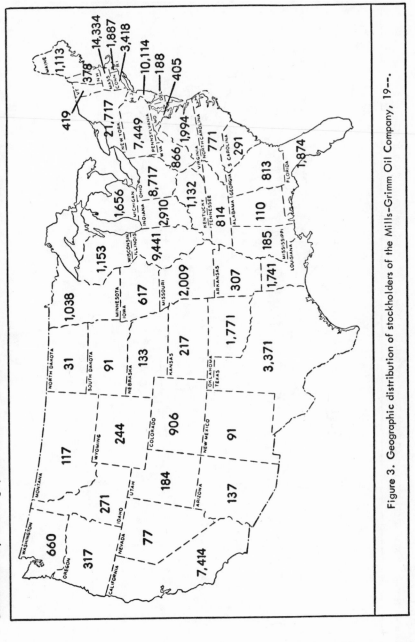

Figure 3. Geographic distribution of stockholders of the Mills–Grimm Oil Company, 19––.

• = $100,000

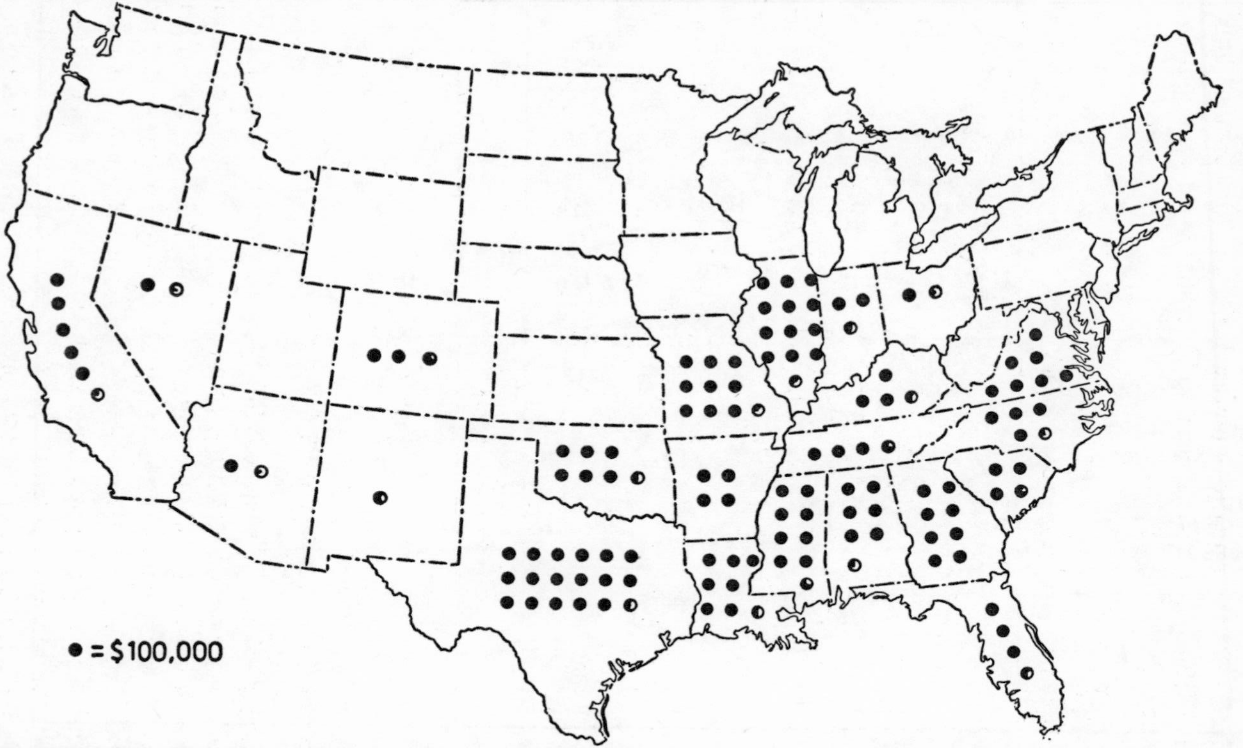

Figure 11. United States sales of Dixie Cola, 19--.

4. Some form of chart may be placed within each geographic area to depict the quantities representative of that area, as illustrated in Figure 7-16. Bar charts and pie charts are commonly used in such illustrations.

FIGURE 7-16
Statistical map showing comparisons by charts within geographic areas

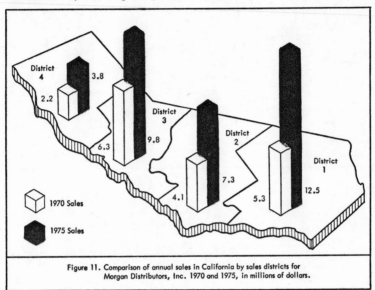

Figure 11. Comparison of annual sales in California by sales districts for Morgan Distributors, Inc. 1970 and 1975, in millions of dollars.

MISCELLANEOUS GRAPHIC AIDS

The graphic aids discussed thus far are those most commonly used. Others are sometimes helpful in assisting in the task of communicating. Photographs and drawings (see Figure 7-17) may sometimes serve a useful communication purpose. Diagrams, too, may help to make simple a complicated explanation or description, particularly when technological procedures are being communicated. Then there are many almost nameless types of graphic presentation—most of which are combinations of two or more of the more common techniques. Since anything in the way of graphic design is acceptable as long as it helps to communicate the true story, the possibilities of graphic-aid design are almost unlimited.

138

FIGURE 7-17
Illustration of a drawing

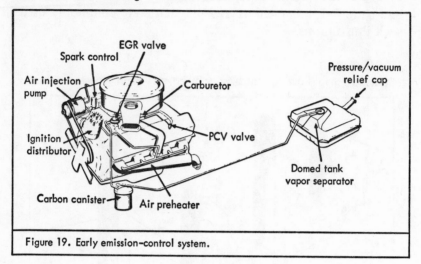

Figure 19. Early emission-control system.

8

Physical presentation of reports

When your reader looks at your report, he sees not only the message you have formed; he sees also the overall appearance of your work. As with the words and illustrations, the appearance of your report becomes a part of the communication he receives and has an effect on the message he forms in his mind.

If, for example, he looks at your work and sees a neat, well-arranged document, a favorable impression is likely to form in his mind. Such favorable impressions probably will make him more receptive to the information in your message. At the other extreme, if he sees an untidy, poorly arranged paper, he is likely to form a negative impression in his mind. And this impression will negatively affect his receptiveness to the information you seek to communicate to him. In other words, the impression of appearance of your work formed in your reader's mind becomes a part of his thinking. Thus, it serves to affect the meanings he gives to the information communicated.

You can do much to insure the communication effect of your report by giving it the typing care and arrangement which will help in your communication effort. Hence, you should make good use of the following guide to the physical arrangement of reports.

GENERAL INFORMATION ON
PHYSICAL PREPARATION

Because your reports are most likely to be typed, you should have a general knowledge of the mechanics involved in manuscript typing. Even if you do not have to type your own reports, you should know enough about report form to make certain that justice is done to your work. You cannot be certain that your report is presented in good form unless you know good form.

Conventional page layout

For the typical text page in the report, a conventional layout is that which appears to fit the page like a picture in a frame (see Figure 8-1). This eye-pleasing layout, however, is arranged to fit the page space not covered by the binding of the report. Thus, you must allow an extra two thirds of an inch or so on the left margins of the pages of a left-bound report and at the top of the pages of a top-bound report.

As a general rule, top, left, and right margins should be equal and uniform. For double-spaced manuscripts, about 1 inch is recommended. From 1¼ to 1½ inches is considered ideal for single-spaced work (see Figure 8-2). Bottom margins are customarily made slightly larger than those at the top—about half again as much. The left margin, of course, is easily marked by the characters which begin the line. The right margin is formed by the average lengths of the full lines. As nearly as possible, this right margin should be kept straight—that is, without dips or bulges.

You may find it advisable to mark off in black ink a rectangle of the size of the layout you are using. Then you may place the rectangle beneath each page as you type, so that you can see the dimensions you are using and can end your typed lines appropriately.

Special page layouts

Certain pages in the text may have individual layouts. Pages displaying major titles (first pages of chapters, tables of contents, synopses, and the like) conventionally have an extra half inch or so of space at the top (see Figure 8-3). This technique has long been followed by publishers and is illustrated in almost all published books.

FIGURE 8-1
Recommended layout for a double-spaced normal page

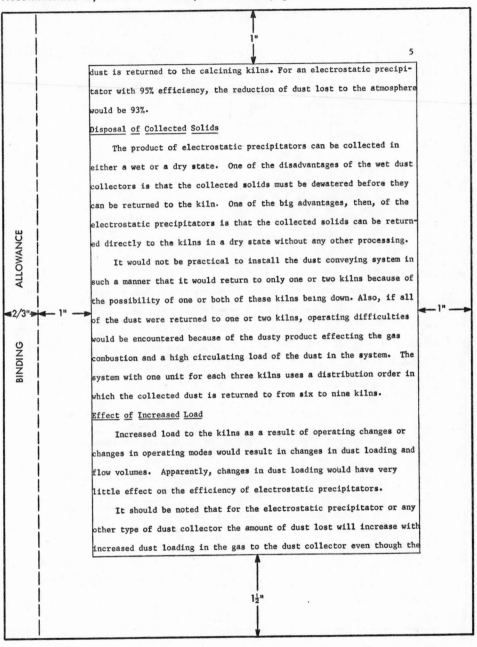

dust is returned to the calcining kilns. For an electrostatic precipitator with 95% efficiency, the reduction of dust lost to the atmosphere would be 93%.

Disposal of Collected Solids

The product of electrostatic precipitators can be collected in either a wet or a dry state. One of the disadvantages of the wet dust collectors is that the collected solids must be dewatered before they can be returned to the kiln. One of the big advantages, then, of the electrostatic precipitators is that the collected solids can be returned directly to the kilns in a dry state without any other processing.

It would not be practical to install the dust conveying system in such a manner that it would return to only one or two kilns because of the possibility of one or both of these kilns being down. Also, if all of the dust were returned to one or two kilns, operating difficulties would be encountered because of the dusty product effecting the gas combustion and a high circulating load of the dust in the system. The system with one unit for each three kilns uses a distribution order in which the collected dust is returned to from six to nine kilns.

Effect of Increased Load

Increased load to the kilns as a result of operating changes or changes in operating modes would result in changes in dust loading and flow volumes. Apparently, changes in dust loading would have very little effect on the efficiency of electrostatic precipitators.

It should be noted that for the electrostatic precipitator or any other type of dust collector the amount of dust lost will increase with increased dust loading in the gas to the dust collector even though the

FIGURE 8-2
Recommended layout for a normal single-spaced page

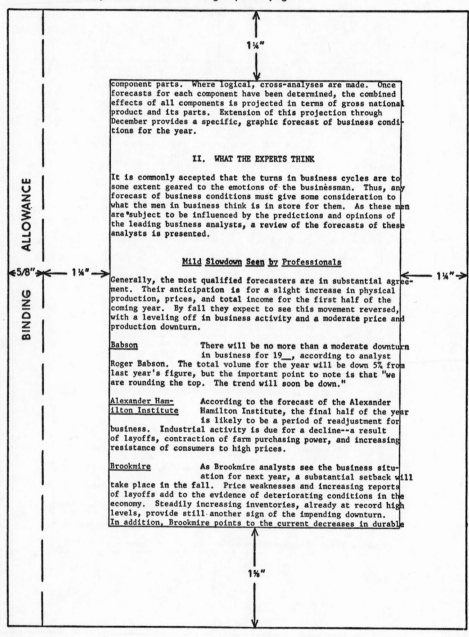

component parts. Where logical, cross-analyses are made. Once forecasts for each component have been determined, the combined effects of all components is projected in terms of gross national product and its parts. Extension of this projection through December provides a specific, graphic forecast of business conditions for the year.

II. WHAT THE EXPERTS THINK

It is commonly accepted that the turns in business cycles are to some extent geared to the emotions of the businessman. Thus, any forecast of business conditions must give some consideration to what the men in business think is in store for them. As these men are subject to be influenced by the predictions and opinions of the leading business analysts, a review of the forecasts of these analysts is presented.

Mild Slowdown Seen by Professionals

Generally, the most qualified forecasters are in substantial agreement. Their anticipation is for a slight increase in physical production, prices, and total income for the first half of the coming year. By fall they expect to see this movement reversed, with a leveling off in business activity and a moderate price and production downturn.

Babson   There will be no more than a moderate downturn in business for 19___, according to analyst Roger Babson. The total volume for the year will be down 5% from last year's figure, but the important point to note is that "we are rounding the top. The trend will soon be down."

Alexander Hamilton Institute   According to the forecast of the Alexander Hamilton Institute, the final half of the year is likely to be a period of readjustment for business. Industrial activity is due for a decline--a result of layoffs, contraction of farm purchasing power, and increasing resistance of consumers to high prices.

Brookmire   As Brookmire analysts see the business situation for next year, a substantial setback will take place in the fall. Price weaknesses and increasing reports of layoffs add to the evidence of deteriorating conditions in the economy. Steadily increasing inventories, already at record high levels, provide still another sign of the impending downturn. In addition, Brookmire points to the current decreases in durable

FIGURE 8-3
Recommended layout for double-spaced page with title displayed

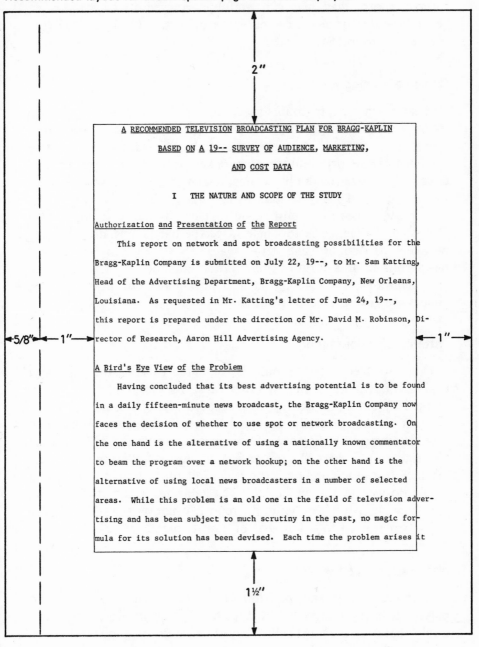

Letters of transmittal and authorization also may have individual layouts. They are typed in any conventional letter form. In more formal reports they may be carefully arranged to have the same general outline or shape as the space upon which they appear (see Figure 8-7, page 154).

Choice of typing form

It is conventional to double-space the typed report. This procedure stems from the old practice of double spacing to make typed manuscripts more easily read by the proofreader and printer. The practice has been carried over into typed work that is not to be further reproduced. Advocates of double spacing claim that it is easy to read, as the reader is not likely to lose his line place.

In recent years the use of single spacing has gained in popularity. The general practice is to single-space the paragraphs, double-space between paragraphs, and triple-space above all centered heads. Supporters of this form of presentation contend that it saves space and facilitates fast reading, as it approximates the printing most people are accustomed to reading.

Patterns of indentation

Double-spaced typing should be indented to show the paragraph beginnings. On the other hand, because its paragraphs are clearly marked by extra line spacing, single-spaced typing is usually blocked.

There is no generally accepted pattern of indentation. Some sources advocate a distance of four spaces; some prefer five, some like eight; and others like ten and more. Any decision as to the best distance to use is purely arbitrary and left up to you, although you would do well to follow the practice established in the office, group, or school for which you write the report. Whatever the selection, the important rule to follow is that of consistency.

Neatness in typed work

Even with the best typewriter available, the finished work is no better than the efforts of the typist. But this statement does not imply that only the most skilled typist can turn out good work. Even the inexperienced typist can produce acceptable manuscripts simply by exercising care.

You should take care in correcting your typing mistakes, for obvious corrections (strikeovers, erasure holes in the page, and the like) stand out in the manuscript like a sore thumb. With a little bit of care, this operation can be done so well that the casual reader doesn't detect the error.

Possibly nothing detracts more from a report than type which the eye must strain to read. So you should take care to see that your typewriter is equipped with a good, black ribbon—one that will make legible letters. A medium-inked ribbon is recommended for most typing work. Because the ink is likely to smear a bit on the first few pages typed with a new ribbon, it may be wise to type really important work only after a ribbon has had the excess ink worn off. Because of the sharp contrast in type it would cause, changing ribbons in the middle of a manuscript should be avoided.

For neat and clearly legible typing, the typefaces must be regularly cleaned. Ink from the ribbon tends to collect and dry in the typefaces. If allowed to remain, it will fill the enclosed portions of the type characters. Smudged or fuzzy typing is the result. Any small brush may be used for this purpose.

Numbering of pages

Two systems of numbers are used in numbering the pages of the written report. Arabic numerals are conventional for the text portion, normally beginning with the first page of the introduction and continuing through the appendix. Small roman numerals are used for the pages preceding the text. Although all of these prefatory pages are counted in the numbering sequence, the numbers generally are not placed on the pages preceding the table of contents.

Placement of the numbers on the page varies with the binding used for the report. In reports which are bound at the top of the page, all page numbers are usually centered at the bottom of the page, a double or triple space below the layout used in the typing.

For the more widely used left-side binding, page numbers are placed in the upper right corner of the page, a double space above the top line of the layout and in line with the right margin. Exception to this placement is customarily made for special-layout pages which have major titles and an additional amount of space displayed at the top. Included in this group may be the first page of the report text; the synopsis; the table of contents; and, in very long and formal works, the first page of each major division or chapter. Numbers for such pages as these are centered a double or triple space below the imaginary line marking the bottom of the layout.

Display of captions

Captions—or headings, as they are sometimes called—are titles to the various divisions of the report. They represent the organization steps worked out previously and are designed to help the reader find his way through this organization plan. Thus, it is important that the captions show the reader at a glance the importance of their part in the report.

This importance of captions may be emphasized in two ways—by type and by position. Any logical combination of type and position may be used to show differences in the importance of captions. In actual practice, however, a few standard orders of captions have become widely used.

There are four major positions of captions, as shown in Figure 8-4. Highest of these four in order of rank is the centered caption. This caption is on a line by itself and is centered between left and right margins. Next in order is the marginal caption. Beginning on the left margin, this caption is also on a line by itself. The box caption is third in this ranking, but it normally is used only in single-spaced copy. It begins on the left margin and is surrounded by a box of space formed by indenting the first few lines of the text. The box indentations are kept of equal width throughout the report, although the heights of the boxes will vary with the number of words in the captions enclosed. Fourth in importance is the run-in caption. This caption simply runs into the first line of the text it covers and is distinguished from the text only by underscoring.

Were the report to be printed, there would be a wide variety of typefaces and sizes that could be used to show different degrees of importance in the captions. But most reports are typed and thereby limited by what type variations can be made with an ordinary typewriter. Except when unusual typefaces are available, the report writer can show type distinctions in only two ways—by the use of capitals and the underscore. Spacing between letters is sometimes used,

FIGURE 8-4
Caption positions in order of importance

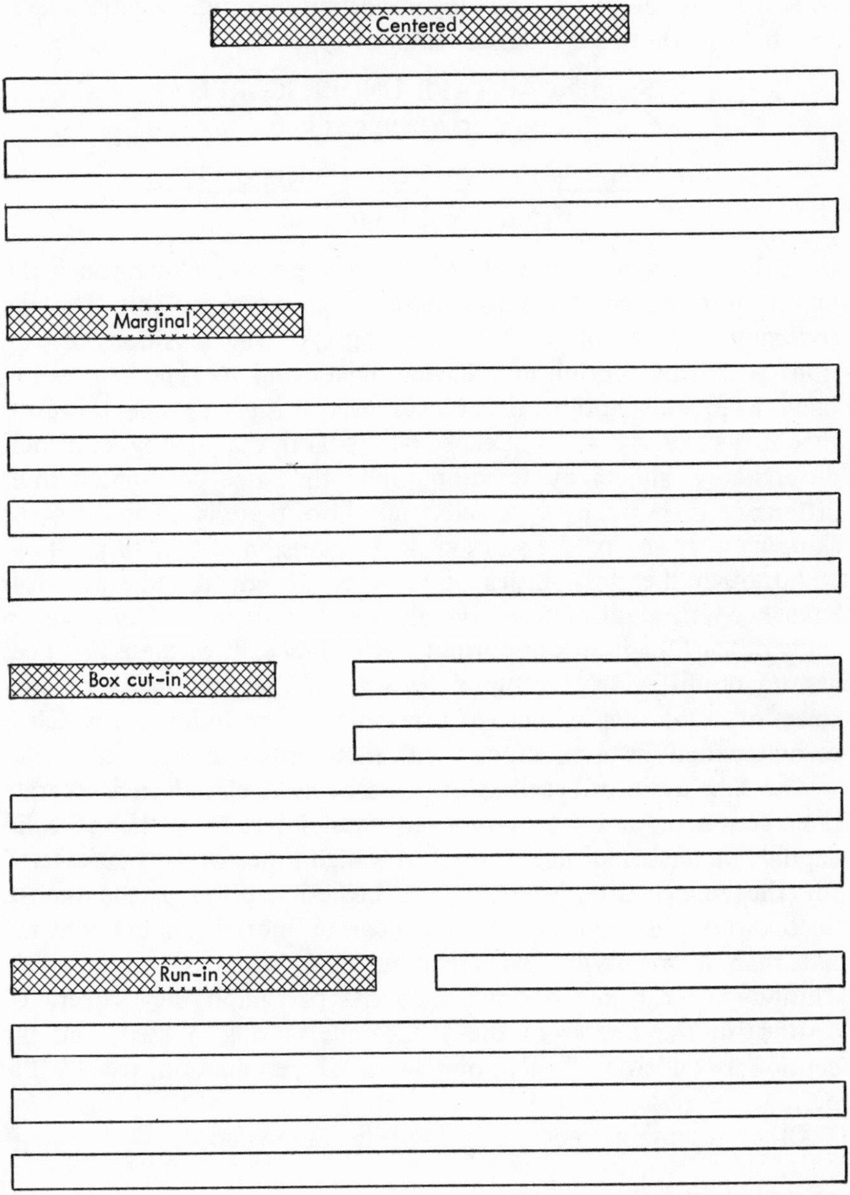

although the space requirements of this technique normally eliminate it from consideration. But even though the report writer is
limited to two means of showing importance by type selection, he is
able to construct four distinct ranks of type:

<u>SOLID CAPITALS UNDERSCORED</u>
SOLID CAPITALS
<u>Capitals</u> <u>and</u> <u>Lowercase</u> <u>Underscored</u>
Capitals and Lowercase

In theory, any combination of type and position which shows the
relative importance of the captions at a glance is acceptable. The one
governing rule to follow in considering types and positions of captions is that no caption may have a higher ranking type or position
than any of the captions of a higher level. It is permissible, however,
that two successive steps of captions appear in the same type, if their
difference is shown by position, or in the same position, if their
difference is shown by type selection. Also, there is no objection to
skipping over any of the steps in the progression of type or position.

Although the possibilities of variation are great, some practices
have become almost conventional, possibly because they excel in
showing each caption's importance at a glance. Too, these practices
are no doubt widely accepted because of their simplicity of construction. One such scheme of captioning is the following, which is
recommended for use in reports with three orders of division.

The first order of captions in this scheme is placed on a separate
line, centered, and typed in solid capital letters. Although solid
capitals underscored may be used, this high type normally is reserved
for the report title, which is the highest caption in the report.
Second-order captions are also on separate lines, beginning with the
left margin and typed with capitals and lowercase underscored.
Third-degree captions are run into the paragraph they cover. To
distinguish the line from the text, underscoring is used, and the
caption is ended with a strong mark of punctuation, usually the
period.

Other acceptable schemes include the following:

1. Centered, solid capitals.
2. Centered, capitals and lowercase underscored.
3. Marginal, capitals and lowercase underscored.
4. Run-in, capitals and lowercase underscored.

1. Centered, solid capitals.
2. Marginal, capitals and lowercase underscored.
3. Box cut-in, capitals and lowercase underscored.
4. Run-in, capitals and lowercase underscored.

1. Centered, solid capitals.
2. Centered, capitals and lowercase underscored.
3. Box cut-in, capitals and lowercase.

1. Centered, solid capitals.
2. Marginal, capitals and lowercase underscored.
3. Box cut-in, capitals and lowercase underscored.

MECHANICS AND FORMAT OF THE REPORT PARTS

The foregoing notes on physical appearance apply generally to all parts of the report. But for the individual construction of the specific report pages, additional special notes are needed. So that you may be able to get and follow these special notes, a part-by-part review of the physical construction of the formal report is given. Much of this presentation is left to illustration, for volumes could be written about the minute details of construction. Major points, however, are indicated.

Title fly

Primarily used in the most formal reports, the title fly contains only the report title. The title is placed slightly above the vertical center of the page in an eye-pleasing arrangement, and all of its lines are centered with regard to left and right margins. It is typed in the highest ranking type used in the report (usually solid capitals underscored) and is double-spaced if more than one line is required.

Title page

The title page normally contains three main areas of identification (Figure 8-5), although some forms present the same information in four or five spots on the page (Figure 8-6). In the typical three-spot title page, the first item covered is the report title. It is best typed in the highest ranking type used in the report, usually solid capitals

FIGURE 8-5
Good layout for the three-spot title page

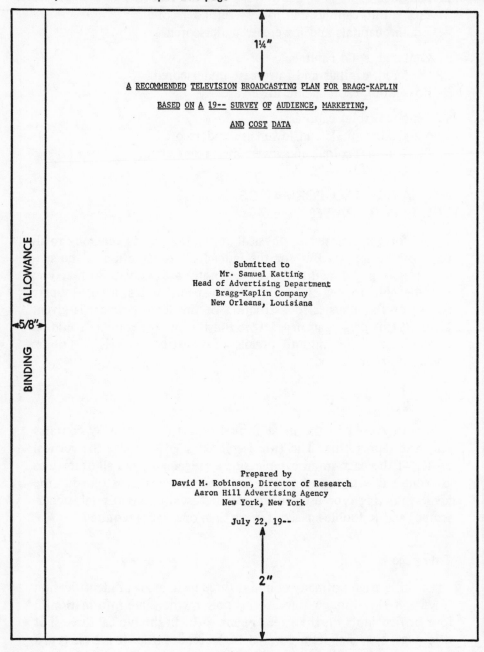

FIGURE 8-6
Good layout for the four-spot title page

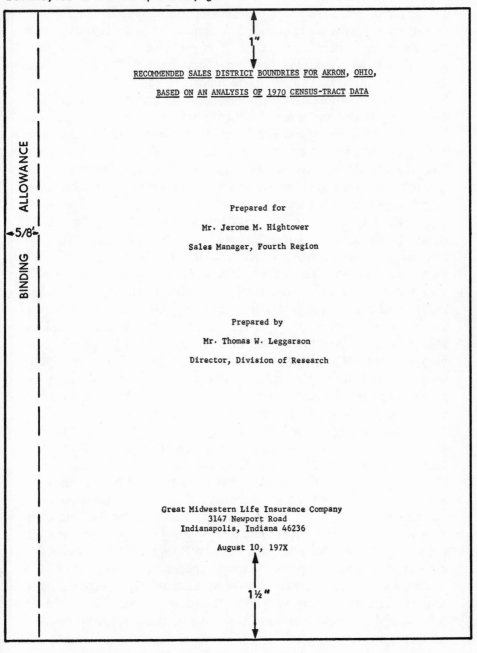

underscored. The title is centered; and if more than one line is required, the lines are broken between thought units, and both lines are centered. The lines are appropriately double-spaced.

The second area of identification names the individual or group for whom the report is prepared. It is preceded by an identifying phrase such as "Prepared for" or "Submitted to"—words which indicate the individual's role in the report. In addition to the name, identification by title or role, company, and address may be included, particularly if the writer and recipient are from different companies. If the information below the identifying phrase requires three or more lines of type, single spacing is recommended; fewer than three lines may be double-spaced. But regardless how this information is spaced, the identifying phrase appears best set off from the facts below it by a double space.

The third area of information identifies the writer of the report. It, too, is preceded by an identifying phrase. "Prepared by," "Written by," or any such wording which describes this person's role in the report may be used. The writer's title or role, company, and address may also be given here. As a final part of this group of information, the date of publication is usually included. This identification information also is single-spaced if four lines are required and double-spaced if it involves three lines or less. Likewise, its identification phrase is set off with a double space. The date line is preferably double-spaced from the information preceding it, regardless of previous spacing. Placement of the three spots of information on the page should conform to an eye-pleasing arrangement.

One such arrangement begins the title about 1¼ inches from the top of the page. The final spot of information is ended about 2 inches from the page bottom. The center spot of information is placed so as to split the space between the top and bottom units in a 2-to-3 ratio, the bottom space being the larger. Line lengths of the information units, of course, are largely governed by the data contained; yet you will have some opportunity to combine or split units. Preferably, the lines will have sufficient length to keep the units from having an overall "skinny" appearance.

The wording of the title should be so carefully selected that it tells at a glance what is covered in the report. That is, it should fit the report like a glove, covering all of the report information snugly— no more, no less.

For completeness of coverage, you may build your title around the five W's of the journalist: *who, what, where, when, why.* Sometimes, *how* may be added to this list. In some problems, however, not all of the *W*'s are essential to complete identification; nevertheless, they serve as a good checklist for completeness. For example, a title of a report analyzing the Lane Company's 197*x* advertising campaigns might be constructed as follows:

Who:	Lane Company
What:	Analysis of advertising campaigns
Where:	Not essential
When:	197*x*
Why:	Implied

Thus the title emerges: "Analysis of the Lane Company's 197*x* Advertising Campaigns."

Obviously, you cannot write a completely descriptive title in a few words—certainly not in a word or two. Extremely short titles are as a rule vague. They cover everything; they touch nothing. Yet it is your objective to achieve conciseness in addition to completeness, so you must also seek the most economical word pattern consistent with completeness. Occasionally, in the attempt to achieve conciseness and completeness at once, it is advisable to make use of subtitles.

Letters of transmittal and authorization

As their names imply, the letters of transmittal and authorization are actual letters. Therefore, they should appear as letters. They may be typed in an acceptable letter form—pure block, modified block, or indented. A layout plan recommended for at least the more formal reports is that which fits the letter into a rectangle of the same shape as the space on which it is typed (see Figure 8-7). This rectangle is marked by the dateline at the top, the initial characters of type at the left, the average of the line lengths at the right, and the last line in the signature at the bottom. For the best optical effect, the rectangle should ride a little high on the page, with a ratio of top margin to bottom margin of about 2 to 3.

Acknowledgments

When the writer is indebted to the assistance of others, it is fitting that the indebtedness be made known somewhere in the report. If the number of individuals involved is small, acknowledgment may be made in the introduction of the report, or in the letter of transmittal.

FIGURE 8-7

Letter of transmittal fitted to the shape of the space in which typed

MIDWESTERN RESEARCH INSTITUTE

3241 MONROE STREET
CHICAGO, ILLINOIS

July 22, 19--

Mr. Joel D. Karp, President
The Munson Company
2121 Oldham Road
Cleveland, Ohio 44103

Dear Mr. Karp:

Here is the recommendation report on Munson's radio advertising policy that you requested in your May 9th letter.

As you read the report, undoubtedly you will be (as I was)
surprised to see the facts point so clearly to one decision.
The simple explanation is that this is one of those instances
in which all pertinent data lead down the same path to one
conclusion.

Perhaps you will want to question the matter of cost analysis.
It's true that the recommended plan is going to cost a bit
more initially. But the long-run outlook is much more positive. If you would like more information on the cost question, let me know and I'll rush it to you.

I am grateful to you for this assignment. And I'll be looking
forward to helping you again with other problems that you
might have.

Sincerely yours,

James W. Worthington
James W. Worthington
Director of Research

JWW:ek

BINDING ALLOWANCE

In the rare event that numerous acknowledgments need to be made, a special section may be constructed. This section is headed with the simple title "Acknowledgments" and is typed with the same layout as any other text page which has a title displayed.

Table of contents

The table of contents is the report outline in its polished, finished form. It lists the major report captions with the page numbers on which these captions appear. Although not all reports require a table of contents, one should be a part of any report long enough for a guide to be helpful to the readers.

The page is appropriately headed by the caption "Contents" or "Table of Contents," as shown in Figure 8-8. The page layout is that used for any report page with a title displayed. Below the title, two columns are set up. One contains the captions, generally beginning with the first report part following the table of contents. The captions may or may not include the outline letters and numbers. If numbers are used, the entries are arranged so that the last digits of compound numbers are aligned. The other column, which is brought over to the right margin and headed by the caption "Page," contains the page numbers on which the captions may be found. These numbers are aligned on their right digits. The two columns are connected by leader lines of periods, preferably with spaces intervening.

As a rule, all captions of the highest level of division are typed with line spaces above and below them. Captions below this level may be uniformly single-spaced or double-spaced, depending on the overall lengths of the captions. If the captions are long, covering most of the line or extending to a second line, uniform double spacing between captions is recommended. Short captions may be typed in consistent single-spaced form. Some authorities, however, prefer double-spacing all of the contents entries when double spacing is used in the text.

In the table of contents, as in the body of the report, variations in the type used to distinguish different levels of captions is permissible. But the contents type variations need not be the same as those used in the text typing. Usually, the highest level of captions is distinguished from the other levels, and sometimes second-degree captions are distinguished from lower captions by type differences. It is not wrong to show no distinction at all by using plain capitals and lowercase throughout.

FIGURE 8-8
Good layout and mechanics in the first page of the table of contents

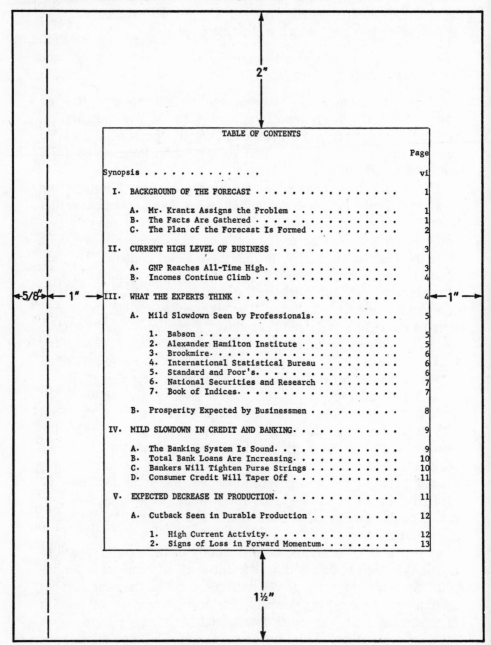

2"

5/8" 1" 1"

1½"

Table of illustrations

The table of illustrations is constructed either as a continuation of the table of contents or as a separate table. This table, as shown in Figure 8-9, lists the graphic aids presented in the report in much the same way as the report parts are listed in the table of contents.

The table is headed with an appropriately descriptive title such as "Table of Charts and Illustrations," or "List of Tables and Charts," and "Table of Figures." If the table is placed on a separate page, the page layout is the same as that for any other text page with title displayed. And if it is placed as a continued part of the table of contents, the table of illustrations is begun after spacing four or more lines from the last contents entry.

The table is made up of two columns—one for the graphic-aid title and the second for the page on which the aid appears. Heading the second column is the caption "Page." The two columns are also connected by leader lines of spaced periods. Line spacing in the table is optional, again depending on the line lengths of the entries. Preceding each entry title appears that entry's number, and should these numbers be roman or otherwise require more than one digit, the digits are appropriately aligned on their right member. In reports where two or more illustration types (tables, charts, maps, etc.) are used, and each has been given its own numbering sequence, the entries may be listed successively by types.

The physical layout requirements of the letter report are the same as those for any other letter. Any conventional letter form may be used; and as was explained in the discussion of layout of the transmittal and authorization letters, the letter report might well approximate the shape of the space in which it is typed.

Memorandum reports, although they are a type of informal letter, do not necessarily follow conventional letter format. The most popular form (see Figure 8-10) uses the military arrangement of introductory information: *To, From, Subject.* Generally, this information is followed by informal presentation of facts in organized fashion. Other forms of the memorandum vary widely. Some resemble questionnaires, in that they are comprised of lists of topics or questions with spaces provided for the written answers. Others are simply handwritten notes on standard interoffice communication forms.

158

FIGURE 8-9
Good layout and mechanics in the last page of the table of contents showing the table
of illustrations attached

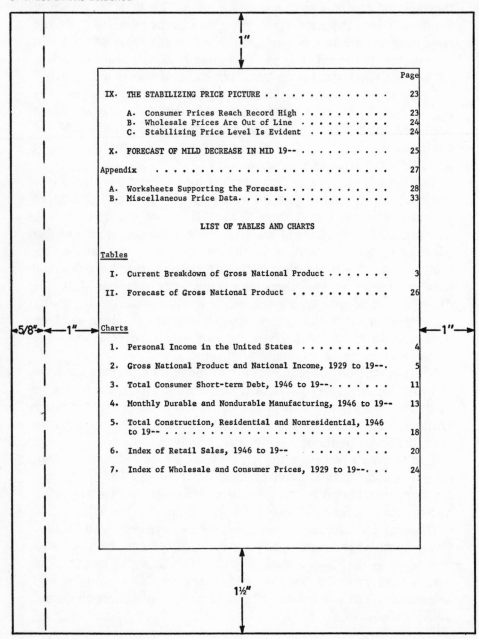

1"

5/8" 1"

1"

1½"

FIGURE 8-10
Good form for a memorandum report

COWAN
CHEMICAL
CO., INC.

MEMORANDUM   June 7, 1974

FROM: R. H. Alton
             Research and Development Department

TO: Horace A. Watson, General Manager
             Conrad H. Ward, Product Development
             John E. Shelton, Chief Chemist
             Library (2)

SUBJECT: Phenol Manufacture by the X Process

SUMMARY AND RECOMMENDATIONS

The findings of this investigation support the recommendation that the X process for making phenol be dropped. In the investigation four methods of removing water from a solution containing 3% phenol and 4.5% HCl were considered. Two of these, spray evaporation and submerged combustion, were found not to be usable. The other two, tower concentration and vacuum evaporation, were found to be workable but not very good.

INTRODUCTION

Authorized by Mr. Horace A. Watson January 17, 1974, an investigation was conducted to evaluate four methods of concentrating a solution of 3% phenol and 4.5% hydrochloric acid obtained in the X process of manufacturing phenol. Previous investigation has indicated that the X process is the only practical process available to the company for making phenol.

The X process consists of passing chlorobenzene vapor and water through a tube maintained at a temperature of about 165°C. From this mixture a solution forms, consisting of about 3.5% phenol, 4.5% hydrochloric acid, and 90% water. Included, also, is a small amount of unreacted chlorobenzene. Previous investigations have worked out all steps in the process except the final one of concentrating the weak phenol solution. Because of the presence of hydrochloric acid, ordinary evaporation equipment cannot be used. This chemical would attack any metal sufficiently inexpensive to use.

DISCUSSION OF RESULTS

In an effort to find a practical solution to the problem, the four possibilities were considered: (1) spray evaporation, (2) submerged combustion, (3) tower concentration, and (4) vacuum evaporation.

FIGURE 8-10 (continued)
Good form for a memorandum report

Spray evaporation was eliminated as a possibility on the advice of Dr. Charles E. Coward, consultant to the company. Dr. Coward advised that the presence of hydrochloric acid constituted an insurmountable obstacle.

The method of submerged combustion consists of operating a gas burner submerged beneath the liquid to be concentrated. When tested in the laboratory this method resulted in a high loss of phenol during the evaporation (see report on Research Project 2143). Since Drake and Bolen Manufacturing Company, manufacturers of submerged equipment, could not suggest any corrective change in equipment, this method was rejected.

The method of concentrating phenol solutions by passing hot combustion gases from propane up a tower against a descending stream of solution was tried (Project 3171). Because of the combustion of phenol, this method proved to be ineffective. Apparently the combustion resulted largely from incomplete wetting of the packing by the small liquid flow. Further trials (Project 3190) attempted to use a recirculating system in order to increase the liquid flow. Yield values gave evidence that a maximum process yield of 90% could be expected by using this method.

The method of vacuum concentration was tried by flashing a hot phenol solution into a steam-jacketed tube maintained at a moderately high vacuum (Project 3011). The method produced a process yield of 96% phenol. This method, however, has the disadvantage of requiring expensive equipment and of possibly giving smaller process yields when carried out in large-scale equipment, since experiment showed that heat-transfer coefficients decreased as the diameter of the tube increased.

CONCLUSIONS AND RECOMMENDATIONS

From the results of these experiments the apparent conclusion is that, of all the methods investigated, only the tower concentration and vacuum evaporation methods are usable. Neither one is particularly good. Of the two, the former is the better. It produces lower yields, but these are compensated for by cheap equipment.

It is therefore recommended that consideration of the X process be dropped.

9

Handling secondary information

Some of the information you use in your reports may come from secondary sources—that is, from books, articles, bulletins, and others. Such information is the product of someone else's work. So when using it in your report, the honest thing to do is to make it clear to your reader that you do not take credit for it. You make this point obvious by following certain conventional procedures. A summary of these procedures follows.

TEXT USE OF SECONDARY INFORMATION

You may use secondary information in either of two ways: (1) you may paraphrase (put it in your own words) or (2) you may quote it verbatim (in the original author's words). Your decision as to whether to quote or paraphrase is largely a judgment matter, and there are arguments for each. Quoted words appear authoritative, and they are more likely to contain the original author's meaning. On the other hand, paraphrased words typically are more economical and better fit the style and purpose of your writing.

Information that you choose to use verbatim should be clearly distinguished from the surrounding text. The conventional practice is to present short (four lines or less) passages in quotation marks and within the report text. Longer quotations (five lines or more) are set apart from the normal text with additional left and right margins (see Figure 9-1). Such passages are single-spaced regardless of the spacing used in the text. They require no quotation marks.

162

FIGURE 9-1

Segment of a report showing mechanics of typing a quoted passage

Professor Morgenstern commented on the Committee's findings

in these words:

> The Committee's report forms a very valuable ad-
> dition to the material available on employment
> statistics and is a fine example of the sort of
> appraisal that needs to be made if users of
> economic statistics are to be sufficiently in-
> formed to make worthwhile use of statistics.[9]

Errors exist in data on unemployment--errors of response,

of definition, and of seasonal adjustment, for example. The

Additional questions of form that you need to answer in handling secondary material are how to insert your own comments and how to show omissions in quoted work. Inserting your comments within quoted passages is easy. You merely enclose your words in brackets. Handling omissions is more involved. As you know, omissions can change the meaning of writing. So you must take care to tell your reader anytime you omit words from a quoted passage. You show omissions by use of ellipsis points (a series of periods, usually three, sometimes typed with intervening spaces) at the point of omission. Three dots are used if the material omitted occurs between the first and last words of a quoted sentence. Four dots—a period for the sentence and three spaced dots—are used if the omission occurs at the end of a sentence. Other punctuation marks may be used with ellipsis points if they give added clarity. The following passage illustrates this technique:

> ... the testing [of the finished coating] cannot be done until after the sealer coat is applied. . . . If the fault found is small, it can be retouched. . . . if large, the coating must be removed by burning.

In long quotations, it is conventional to show omissions of a paragraph or more in either of two ways. One way is to show the omission by a full line of dots. The other is to end the paragraph preceding the omission with four ellipsis points.

CONSTRUCTION OF SOURCE FOOTNOTES

As great importance customarily is placed on the honesty of your report and the validity of the information in it, you should inform your reader of the sources of the secondary information used. You may do this in either of two ways—by explanation in the text or by source footnotes. Explanations in the text normally are used only for general references to sources of authority and not for references to specific passages or pages in published material. For the more specific references, footnotes are the rule.

When to footnote

Your decision to use source footnotes should be based on two primary considerations: (1) giving credit where credit is due, and (2) lending the support of authority to the information. Giving credit where it is due clearly is a matter of honesty and courtesy. When work is not yours, it is morally right that you tell your reader whose it is and where it can be found. The value of lending authoritative support to the information should be equally clear. Who is responsible for the information often determines the believability of the information. For example, data collected by the United States Department of Commerce would tend to be more convincing than that gathered by Will Glutz, private businessman.

Following the reasoning of giving credit where it is due, it is apparent that all material quoted should be footnoted. Such words obviously are the contribution of someone other than you. Failure to conform to this practice is to commit plagiarism—the highest crime among writers.

Paraphrased material, also, usually is footnoted. You may make exception to this practice, however, when the material used is general knowledge in the field and is not the contribution of one particular group or person. The decision in such cases is yours to make. If ever you are in doubt, you would be wise to play it safe and footnote.

Placement of the footnote

The most favored placement for the footnote is at the page bottom, separated from the text by a one and one-half inch or two-inch line which begins at the left margin. This placement is most convenient for the reader, for he can read the footnote with a minimum of effort. He does not have to turn pages, as some other placements require; thus, he is not likely to break the continuity of his reading or to lose his place. Because bottom-of-page placement requires that the typist stop typing high enough on the page to allow the footnote to fit inside the page layout, typists frequently do not like this arrangement.

A second placement of the footnote is within the text and as near as possible to the spot of citation. Typically, the note is set off from the text by top and bottom lines which extend the full width of the page. This technique is convenient to the reader, and obviously it pleases the typist.

Also gaining in popularity is a third practice—that of placing all footnotes at the end of the manuscript (or at the ends of chapters in longer works). This form clearly benefits the typist, for it simplifies the typing work. For the reader, however, it is most inconvenient. It requires that he turn pages each time he chooses to read a foot-note. Although the form is gaining in popularity, it is hard to justify it for business use. In business reporting, one of your major objec-tives is to save the valuable time of your reader. This practice simply does not do that.

When you use bottom-of-page placement, the footnote appears below the separating lines. Always it is single-spaced, even though the text may be double-spaced. When you have more than one entry together, you double-space between them. If your text is typed in block form (as it may be if single spacing is used), you also block the footnotes. And if you use indented form (this is the rule with conventional double spacing), you indent the footnotes.

You should key the footnotes with their text references by means of superscripts, which are arabic numerals placed a half line above the normal line. These numbers should appear in the text directly after the last typed character or punctuation mark in the word or words cited. You may number the superscripts consecutively throughout the paper; or you may begin a new series with each chapter or with each page.

Variation in footnote makeup

Unfortunately, there is no one generally accepted footnote form for you to follow. Variations occur from company to company, from department to department, and from authority to authority. Thus, the procedures outlined below cannot be in conformity with all of these groups. But they are generally accepted, and as you will see, they are simple and easy to follow. These simple and easy-to-follow arrangements have two forms—one to be used when there is a bibliography appended to the paper and the other to be used when no bibliography is present.

Footnote form with a bibliography

When you have a bibliography in your report, the footnote references need contain only these parts: (1) author's surname; (2) title of the article, bulletin, book; and (3) page number.

[3] Wilson, *The Report Writer's Guide*, p. 44. (Book reference)

[4] Allison, "Making Routine Reports Talk," p. 71. (Periodical reference)

Should the reader want to know more about the source cited, he may turn to the bibliography. It is your option, however, to use the complete footnote entry, regardless of the presence of a bibliography.

Form of the footnote
without a bibliography

When your paper has no bibliography, you must make a complete footnote for all first references to a source. But, as shown on p. 170, you may shorten repeated references to the same source. Because complete references to books, periodicals, articles, and such differ on certain points of content, we shall review footnote instructions on each of these types separately. All the items that could possibly be placed in each type of entry are listed in the order of arrangement. But not all of these items are always available or essential to a footnote. When you do not have an item, you simply pass over it. In other words, the following lists are intended to give the maximum content and the order of arrangement of the footnote entries. You use only the parts that are available and appropriate. In the simplified procedure recommended here, you use only the comma to separate the entries and a period to end the listing. You may use abbreviations if you are consistent.

Book entry.
1. Superscript. (Arabic numeral keyed with the text reference and placed before the first part of the entry without spacing.)
2. Name of the author, in normal order. (If two or more authors are involved, all may be presented. If the number of authors is too great to list, the first author followed by the Latin *et al.* or its English equivalent "and others" may be used.)
3. Capacity of the author. (Needed only when contribution to the publication is not truly that of the author, such as *editor, translator,* or *compiler.*)
4. Chapter name. (Necessary only in rare instances when the chapter name helps the reader to find the source, such as in references to encyclopedias.)
5. Book name. (Book names are placed in italics. In typewritten work, italics are indicated by underscoring or by solid caps.)
6. Edition. (Only if other than a first edition.)
7. Publishing company.
8. Location of publisher. (If more than one office, one nearest the writer should be included. United States cities alone are sufficient if population exceeds 500,000; city and state are best given for smaller places.)
9. Date. (Year of publication. If revised, year of latest revision.)
10. Page or pages. (Specific page or inclusive pages on which the cited material is found.)

Examples:

(A typical book.) [1]Roger M. D'Aprix, *How's That Again?* Dow Jones-Irwin, Inc., Homewood, Ill., 1972, pp. 87-88.

(A book written by a staff of writers under the direction of an editor. Chapter title is considered helpful.) [2]Alan Durkee and Clyde W. Warren, editors, "Inventory Control," *Encyclopedia of Accounting,* Worrell-Kerr Publishing Company, Inc., New York, 1974, p. 643.

(Book written by a number of co-authors.) [3]Thomas A. Cannon and others, *Experimental Electronics,* Technological Publications, Inc., Los Angeles, 1974, p. 137.

Periodical entry.
1. Superscript.
2. Author's name. (Frequently no author is given. In such cases, the

entry may be skipped, or if it is definitely known to be anonymous, the word "anonymous" may be placed in the entry.)
3. Article name. (Typed in quotation marks.)
4. Periodical name. (Placed in italics, which are made by underscoring typed work.)
5. Publication identification. (Volume number in consistent arabic
or roman numbers, followed by specific date of publication in
parentheses.)
6. Page or pages.

Examples:

[1]Mary E. Tarver, "Ethics of Science," *Science Review,* Vol. 147
(November 7, 1974), pp. 39-40.
[2]Howard E. Howard, "Environmental Concerns and Technological
Growth," *Journal of Industry,* Vol. 15 (August 17, 1972), p. 35.
[3]Jerome E. Shannon, "The Mechanical Design of Physical Instruments,"
The Instrument Journal, December 1973, p. 79.

Newspaper article.
1. Superscript.
2. Source description. (If article is signed, give author's name. Otherwise, give description of article, such as "United Press Dispatch"
or "editorial.")
3. Main head of article. (Subheads not needed.)
4. Newspaper name. (City and state names inserted in brackets if
place names do not appear in newspaper title. State names not
needed in case of very large cities, such as New York, Chicago,
and Los Angeles.)
5. Date of publication.
6. Page. (May even include column number.)

Examples:

[1]United Press Dispatch, "Rival Unions Sign Pact," *The* [Baton Rouge,
Louisiana] *Morning Advocate,* September 3, 1973, p. 1-A.
[2]Editorial, "The North Moves South," *The Austin* [Texas] *American,*
October 3, 1974, p. 2-A.

Letters or documents.
1. Nature of communication.
2. Name of writer.   } With identification by title and organization
3. Name of recipient. } where helpful.
4. Date of writing.
5. Where filed.

Example:

[1]Letter from J. W. Wells, President, Wells Equipment Co., to James Mattoch, Secretary-Treasurer, Southern Industrialists, Inc., June 10, 1974, filed among Mr. Mattoch's personal records.

The types of entries discussed in the preceding paragraphs are those you are most likely to use; yet you are likely to find many unusual types in any extensive research project. Government publications, bulletins, special publications of learned societies, essays, and the like may afford countless special problems. Although you may find help for such special cases in the various books available on style, usually you can work the problem logically. You can do this by keeping in mind that your objective in constructing the footnote is to make it possible for your reader to find the cited source should he choose to do so. As a rule, you will profit by classifying each problem source as either a book or a periodical, depending on which it appears to approximate. Then, you should attempt to construct the appropriate entry, leaving out the parts you feel do not help to identify the source, and inserting any additional information you feel should be included for completeness.

Example:

A writer wants to cite a paper read at the 1974 annual meeting of the Academy of Environmental Sciences held at the University of Washington, Seattle, and published in the proceedings of the meeting. The paper was by Eugene E. Vorman, president of the engineering consulting firm of Vorman and Associates. The reference is to page 176 of the proceedings. As the published proceedings are printed in what appears to approach periodical form (it contains a number of articles and is published annually), the following entry would be appropriate:

[7]Eugene E. Vorman, "Ethics Revisited," *Proceedings of the 1974 Annual Meeting of the Academy of Environmental Sciences,* held and sponsored by the University of Washington, Seattle, p. 176.

Double sources

Sometimes, you will need to cite a passage written by someone other than the author whose name appears in the work consulted. The passage may be a quotation that the author of the consulted work may have borrowed from another author. Or it may be that the source is a collection of papers written by various people and only edited by the one whose name appears on the publication (such as a book of readings). In such cases, the usual procedure is to make what amounts to a double reference. First is the true author's name and the identification of his work (as much as is available). Next are some appropriate relating words, such as "as quoted in" or "cited in." Finally, there is the description of the reference in which the passage was found.

Example:

[3]John W. Benning, "How Green Were the Years," presidential address, 13th annual meeting, Academy of Social Sciences, Boulder, Colorado, 1972, as cited in Henry A. Tucker, *New Concepts in the Social Sciences*, Walthrup Press, Inc., New York, 1974, p. 314.

Standard reference forms

If it becomes necessary to cite a source more than once in a manuscript, as it frequently does, you may keep repetition to a minimum by using certain standard reference abbreviations. Although these abbreviations serve a worthwhile purpose in their attempt to simplify footnote construction, it is unfortunate that they are of Latin origin and, therefore, understood primarily in scholarly circles. Because these forms are so little known, many writers prefer not to use them, even at the expense of repeating full footnote entries. Many publishers as well as writers have adopted the use of shortened, or short form, references following the first citation of a work, in preference to the Latin abbreviations—although some retain the simple *idem*. The short form consists of only the last name of the author and a shortened title of the book, in italics, followed by the page number of the reference. Still, you should understand and be able to use at least the more common of the Latin abbreviations.

Ibid. (ibidem). Literally, *ibid.* means "in the same place." It is used to refer the reader to the preceding footnote, but to a different page. The entry consists of the superscript, *ibid.*, and the page number.

Op. cit. (opere citato). Meaning "in the work cited," this form is used to refer to a previously cited footnote, but not the one directly preceding. That is, the two similar citations are separated by at least one intervening footnote to another source. The entry consists of the superscript, last name of the author, *op. cit.*, and page number.

Loc. cit. (loco citato). This form means "in the place cited," and its use follows its literal meaning. The form is used to refer to a preceding entry, either the one directly preceding or one farther back in the footnote series. It is used only when the page numbers of the two references to the same source are the same. If the entry refers to the footnote directly preceding, *loc. cit.* alone is used. If the form is used to refer to an entry farther back in the series, the author's last name plus *loc. cit.* make up the entry.

The following series of entries illustrates these possibilities.

[1]James Smith, *How to Write the Annual Report,* Small-Boch, Inc., Chicago, p. 173.

[2]*Ibid.,* p. 143. (Refers to Smith's book but to different page.)

[3]William Curtis, "An Experiment with Records," *Business Leader,* Vol. 19 (Dec. 5, 1970), p. 28.

[4]Smith, *op. cit.,* p. 103. (Refers to Smith's book but to different page than in footnote 2.)

[5]Curtis, *loc. cit.* (Refers to Curtis's article and to same page as in footnote 3.)

[6]*Loc. cit.* (Refers to Curtis's article and to same page as in footnotes 3 and 5.)

Other abbreviation forms are frequently used in footnote entries. Some of these are particularly useful in making reference to text passages or to other footnotes. Such references are generally made in discussion footnotes, which are quite different from the source footnotes discussed in the preceding pages. The most widely used of these abbreviations are as follows.

Cf.—compare (directs reader's attention to another passage).
Cf. ante—compare above.
Cf. post—compare below.
ed.—edition.
e.g.—for example.
et al.—and others.
et passim—and at intervals throughout the work.
et seq.—and the following.
i.e.—that is.
idem—the same.
infra—below.
l., ll.—line, lines.
Ms., Mss.—manuscript, manuscripts.
n.d.—no date.
n.n.—no name.
n.p.—no place.

p., pp.—page, pages.
f., ff.—following page, pages.
supra—above.
vol., vols.—volume, volumes.

Discussion footnotes

In sharp contrast with source footnotes are the discussion foot-notes. Through the use of discussion footnotes, you may strive to explain a part of your text, to amplify discussion on a phase of your presentation, to make cross-references to other parts of the paper, and the like. This material is not placed in the text principally be-cause it would tend to slow down or complicate the presentation. But care should be taken so that not too much of the writing is relegated to a subordinate role in footnotes. Material presented in footnote form obviously does not receive the emphasis that material presented in text form receives. Thus, unless you use discretion in selecting the points for footnote presentation, the major story of the paper will suffer.

No standard form could possibly be devised for presentation of the discussion footnote. Naturally, the note should be as concise and clear as you can make it. But general instructions can go no further than these points, for each footnote differs because of content. These examples illustrate some possibilities of this footnote type.

(Cross-reference.)   [1] See the principle of focal points on page 97.

(Amplification of discussion and cross-reference.)   [2] Lee Roy Richards agrees with this conclusion: "The solution to porosity problems such as this is to improve the flow of gas and allow a better envelope of argon to form around the arc and weld puddle." See *Welder's Manual,* p. 143.

(Comparison.)   [3] Contrast with 1970 world crude oil consump-tion of approximately 87 million barrels per day.

MAKEUP OF THE BIBLIOGRAPHY

A bibliography is an orderly list of published material on a par-ticular subject. In a formal paper, the list covers writings on the sub-ject of the paper. The entries in this list closely resemble source footnotes, but the two must not be confused.

The bibliography normally appears as an appended part of a paper and follows the appendix. A fly page containing the one word "Bibliography" in capital letters normally precedes it. The main caption "Bibliography," usually typed in solid capital letters, also heads the page that begins the listings. Below this title, the publications are presented by broad groups and in alphabetical order within the groups. Usually, such groupings as books, periodicals, and bulletins are used. But the determination of groups should be based solely on the types of publications collected in each bibliography. If, for example, a bibliography includes a large number of periodicals and government publications plus a wide assortment of diverse publication types, the bibliography could be divided into three parts: periodicals, government publications, and miscellaneous publications.

As with footnotes, variations in bibliography form are numerous. A simplified form recommended for business use follows the same procedure as that described above for source footnotes, with four major exceptions.

1. The author's name is listed in reverse order, surname first, for the purpose of alphabetizing. If coauthors are involved, however, only the first name is reversed.

2. The entry is generally typed in hanging indention form. That is, the second and all following lines of an entry begin some uniform distance (usually about five spaces) to the right of the beginning point of the first line. The purpose of this indented pattern is to make the alphabetized first line stand out.

3. The bibliography entry gives the inclusive pages of the publication and does not refer to any one page or passage.

4. Second and subsequent references to publications of the same author are indicated by a uniform line (see bibliography illustration). In typed manuscripts, this line may be formed by the underscore struck 10 consecutive times. But this line may be used only if the entire authorship is the same in the consecutive publications. For example, the line could not be used when consecutive entries have one common author but different coauthors.

An illustration of a bibliography is as follows.

BIBLIOGRAPHY
Books

Baxter, Edward O., *A Computer Approach to Decision Models,* Pierpoint Press, Inc., New York, 1974, 381 pp.
Buffa, Elwood S., *Modern Production Management,* 3rd ed., John Wiley and Sons, Inc., New York, 1969, 576 pp.

Hertz, David B., *The Theory and Practice of Industrial Research*, McGraw-Hill Book Company, Inc., New York, 1950, 385 pp.

Moore, Franklin G., *Manufacturing Management*, 5th ed., Richard D. Irwin, Inc., Homewood, Ill., 1969, 567 pp.

Perlick, Walter W. and Raymond V. Lesikar, *Introduction to Business: A Societal Approach*, Business Publications, Inc., Dallas, 1972, 685 pp.

Government publications

United States Bureau of the Census, "Characteristics of the Population," *Nineteenth Census of the United States: Census of Population*, Vol. II, Part 18, United States Government Printing Office, Washington, D.C., 1971, 248 pp.

———, *Statistical Abstract of the United States*, United States Government Printing Office, Washington, D.C., 1970, 1056 pp.

United States Department of Commerce, *Business Statistics: 1971*, United States Government Printing Office, Washington, D.C., 1971, 309 pp.

———, *Survey of Current Business: 1970 Supplement*, United States Government Printing Office, Washington, D.C., 1970, 271 pp.

Periodicals

Day, George S. and David A. Aaker, "A Guide to Consumerism," *Journal of Marketing*, Vol. 34 (July 1970), pp. 12-19.

Holsclaw, J. Walter, "The Emerging Pattern of EDP," *Harvard Business Review*, Vol. 56, No. 2 (March-April 1974), pp. 71-75.

———, "Business Reexamines the Computer," *Computer Science Journal*, Vol. 11, May 1973, pp. 144-49.

Miscellaneous publications

Bradford, Ernest S., *Survey and Directory, Marketing Research Agencies in the United States*, Bureau of Business Research, College of the City of New York, 1972, 137 pp.

Eckard, Fulwar D., *Trends in Computer Usage*, 1950-75, Bulletin No. 543, Division of Engineering Research, University of Idaho, Boise, 1975, 43 pp.

Reference Sources on Chain Stores, Institute of Distribution, Inc., New York, 1970, 116 pp.

STRUCTURE OF THE ANNOTATED BIBLIOGRAPHY

Sometimes, especially in scholarly writing, each bibliography entry is followed by a brief comment on the value and content of the entry. That is, the bibliography is annotated. Such bibliographies are designed to do more than list sources. They have the additional role of helping others who may conduct research on the subject. No definite rules may be given for the composition of the annotation. The comments should, in as brief a fashion as is practical, point out the content and value of each entry. Short descriptive phrases are generally used rather than complete sentences, although sentences are acceptable. The annotation, like the bibliography entry, is single-spaced, but it is separated from the entry by a double space. It, too, is indented from the initial line of the entry, as illustrated below.

Donald, W. T., editor, *Handbook of Business Administration,* McGraw-Hill Book Co., New York, 1971, 731 pp.

Contains a summary of the activities in each major area of business. Written by foremost authorities in each field. Particularly useful to the business specialist who wants a quick review of the whole of business.

Brown, Stanley M., and Lillian Doris, editors, *Business Executive's Handbook,* 3rd ed., 1947, 644 pp.

Provides answers to most routine executive problems in explicit manner and with good examples. Contains good material on correspondence and sales letters.

Appendix A

Illustration of a long formal report

The illustration which appears in the following pages typifies the long, formal report. Although this report is competently constructed and well illustrates this traditional form, it is not submitted as a model in all respects. Because of the need to disguise the names of the branded products involved, perhaps the report has lost some of its realism. Nevertheless, it represents an orderly, thorough, and objective solution to a somewhat complex problem.

RECOMMENDATIONS FOR 197- REPLACEMENTS

IN ALLIED DISTRIBUTORS, INC., SALES FLEET

BASED ON A COMPARISON OF FOUR SUBCOMPACT AUTOMOBILES

RECOMMENDATIONS FOR 197- REPLACEMENTS

IN ALLIED DISTRIBUTORS, INC., SALES FLEET

BASED ON A COMPARISON OF FOUR SUBCOMPACT AUTOMOBILES

Prepared for

Mr. Norman W. Bigbee, Vice-President
Allied Distributors, Inc.
3131 Speedall Street, Akron, Ohio 44302

Prepared by

George W. Franklin, Associate Director
Midwestern Research, Inc.
1732 Midday Avenue, Chicago, Illinois 60607

April 13, 197-

MIDWESTERN RESEARCH, INC.
1732 Midday Avenue
Chicago, Illinois
60607

April 13, 197-

Mr. Norman W. Bigbee
Vice-President in Charge of Sales
Allied Distributors, Inc.
3131 Speedall Street
Akron, Ohio 44302

Dear Mr. Bigbee:

In your hands is the report on the four makes of
subcompact automobiles you asked me to compare last
January 3.

To aid you in deciding which of the four makes you
should buy as replacements for your fleet, I gathered what I believe to be the most complete information available. Much of the operating information
comes from your own records. The remaining data are
the findings of both consumer research engineers and
professional automotive analysts. Only my analyses
of these data are subjective.

I sincerely hope, Mr. Bigbee, that my analyses will
aid you in making the correct decision. I truly
appreciate this assignment. And should you need any
assistance in interpreting my analyses, please call
on me.

Sincerely yours,

George W. Franklin

George W. Franklin
Associate Director

TABLE OF CONTENTS

LIST OF TABLES AND CHARTS

<u>Epitome</u>

That SC-C is the best buy for Allied Distributors, Inc.,
in replacing its present sales fleet is the recommendation of this study. Authorized by Mr. Norman W. Bigbee,
Vice-President, on January 3, 197-, this recommendation
is submitted on April 13, 197-, to give the company an
insight into the problem of replacing the approximately
50 two-year-old subcompact cars in its present sales
fleet. The basis for this recommendation is an analysis
of cost, safety, and construction factors of four makes
of subcompact cars (SC-A, SC-B, SC-C, and SC-D).

The four cars do not show a great deal of difference in
ownership cost (initial cost less trade-in allowance after two years). On a per-car basis, SC-B costs $919 for
two years, which is $106 under SC-C, $168 under SC-A,
and $181 below SC-D. These differences become more mean-
ingful, however, when interpreted in terms of a 50-car
fleet purchase. A purchase of 50 SC-B's would save $5,300
over SC-C, $8,400 over SC-A, and $9,050 over SC-D. Operating costs, however, favor SC-C. Its cost-per-mile
estimate is $0.04001 as compared with $0.04158 for SC-A,
$0.04224 for SC-D, and $0.04338 for SC-B. A composite
of all costs for 50 cars over the two years the cars
would be used shows SC-C to be least costly at $110,027.
SC-A is second with a cost total of $114,345; SC-D is
third with $116,160; and SC-B is the most expensive with
a cost figure of $119,295.

On the qualities that pertain to driving safety, SC-C is
again superior to the other cars. It has the best brakes
of the group and is tied with SC-A for the best weight
distribution. It is second in acceleration and is again
tied with SC-A for the number of standard safety devices.
SC-A is second over-all in this category, having the second best brakes of the group. SC-B is last here because
of its poor acceleration and poor brakes.

Construction features and handling abilities place SC-C
all by itself. It scores higher than any of the other
cars in every category. SC-A and SC-D are tied for second place here, and again SC-B is last, having poor steering and handling qualities.

RECOMMENDATIONS FOR 197- REPLACEMENTS

IN ALLIED DISTRIBUTORS, INC., SALES FLEET

BASED ON A COMPARISON OF FOUR SUBCOMPACT AUTOMOBILES

I. ORIENTATION TO THE PROBLEM

A. The Authorization Facts

This comparison of the qualities of four brands of subcompact automobiles is submitted April 13, 197-, to Mr.
Norman W. Bigbee, Vice-President, Allied Distributors,
Inc. Authorized by Mr. Bigbee at a meeting in his office
January 3, 197-, this investigation has been made under
the direction of George W. Franklin, Associate Director
of Midwestern Research, Inc.

B. Problem of Selecting Fleet Replacements

The objective of this study is to determine which model
of subcompact automobile Allied Distributors, Inc.,
should select for replacements in its sales fleet. The
Company's policy is to replace all two-year-old models
in its sales fleet annually, and approximately fifty automobiles will be replaced this year.

As the replacements involve a major capital outlay, and
as the sales fleet expenses constitute a major sales cost,
the proper selection of a new model presents an important problem. The model selection must be economical, de-
pendable, and safe. Allied is considering four subcompact automobiles as replacement possibilities. As instructed by Mr. Bigbee, for reasons of information secur-
ity, they are identified in this report only as SC-A
(Subcompact A), SC-B, SC-C, and SC-D.

1

2

C. Reports and Records as Sources of Data

The selection of the replacement brand is based on a
comparative analysis of the merits of the four makes.
Data for the comparisons were obtained from both company records and statistical reports. Operating records
of ten representative cars of each make provide information on operating costs. These reports are summaries
compiled by salesmen-drivers and represent actual performance of company cars under daily selling conditions.
Additional material enumerating safety features, over-
all driving quality, and dependability was acquired from
the reports of the Consumers Union of United States, Inc.,
Automotive Industries, and Bond Publishing Company's periodical, Road and Track. Mr. Bigbee furnished the trade-
in allowances granted on the old models. From this material extensive comparisons of the four makes are presented.

D. A Preview to the Presentation

The findings of this report are presented in logical order. Comparative analyses treat three major fields:
operating costs, safety features, and total performance.
Operating costs constitute the major consideration in
comparison and therefore command primary attention.
This category is broken down into single cost areas with
comparisons of the four makes in each area. The most
efficient and economical make in each area is specified.

Safety features constitute the second field of comparison. Again the field is subdivided into single areas,
and the outstanding automobile in each area is noted.
Finally, the total performance and durability of the four
makes is considered. Throughout the report graphic displays emphasize particular comparisons and analyses.

In reaching a final recommendation, the outstanding qualities of each make are summarized, and the four makes are
objectively compared. This comparison serves as the basis for the final conclusion and recommendation.

II. THE MAJOR FACTOR OF COST

Conceivably, an adequate and logical breakdown of the
problem should be followed; and it is, therefore, natural
to begin with cost. First interest is in original cost,

"What is the fleet discount price?" Of second interest in a natural thinking process are the cash differences after trade-in allowances for the old cars. These figures clearly indicate the cash outlay for the new fleet.

A. Initial Costs Favor SC-B

From Table I it is evident that SC-B has the lowest window sticker price before and after trade-in allowances. It has a $181 margin which must be considered in the light of what features are standard on SC-B in comparison with those standard on the other cars. That is, the SC-B may have fewer standard features included in its original cost and, therefore, not be worth as much as the SC-A, SC-C, or SC-D.

TABLE I ORIGINAL COST OF FOUR BRANDS OF SUBCOMPACT CARS IN 197-			
Make	Window sticker prices	Trade-in value for two-year-old makes*	Cash costs after trade-in allowance
SC-A	$2,091	$1,004	$1,087
SC-B	1,919	1,000	919
SC-C	2,040	1,015	1,025
SC-D	2,200	1,100	1,100

*Trade-in value for SC-A and SC-B are estimates
Sources: Primary and Road and Track

It is clear that where features are listed as standard they do not add to original cost, but where listed as options they do. As will be shown in a later table, the SC-D has many more standard features than do the other makes. In addition to a study of standard features, a close look at trade-in values and operating costs will also be necessary to properly evaluate original cost.

4

Further discussion of these facets will be postponed until they are fitted into our comprehensive study of safety
features and operation cost-per-mile estimate.

B. Trade-in Values Show Uniformity

As a logical follow-up of original cost, trade-in values
usually offer some conclusive data for consideration.
Trade-in values are the variable in determining original
cost when stripped prices are fairly uniform. In this
study the trade-in values are fairly uniform, varying
only by $100 from highest of $1,100 for the SC-D to lowest of $1,000 for the SC-B (Table I).

Although fairly uniform, these figures appear to be more
significant when converted to total amounts involved in
the fleet purchases. A fleet of 50 SC-B's would cost
$45,950. The same fleet of SC-C's, SC-A's, and SC-D's
would cost $51,250, $54,350, and $55,000 respectively.
Thus, $5,300 could be saved by purchasing SC-B's over
SC-C's; $8,400 could be saved in relation to SC-A's; and
$9,050 could be saved when compared to SC-D's.

C. Operating Costs Are Lowest for SC-C

SC-C has the lowest maintenance cost of the four, .00563
cents per mile; but SC-D is close behind with .00590 cents.
Both of these are well below the SC-B and SC-A figures of
.00781 and .00789 respectively. The components of these
values, as shown in Table II, are estimates of repairs and
resulting loss of working time, miscellaneous, and tire
replacements.

It should be stressed here how greatly repair expense
influences the estimates. Actually, two expenses are involved, for to the cost of repairs must be added the expense of lost time by the salesmen. Obviously, a salesman without a car is unproductive. Each hour lost by car
repairs adds to the cost of the car's operation.

As shown in Table II, the hours lost per repair for each
make are the same (five hours). Thus, the important consideration is the number of repairs and the costs of these
repairs. On this basis, the SC-C has the lowest total
cost burden at $310. SC-D ranks second with $325. SC-B
is third with $430, and SC-A is last with $434.

5

TABLE II
COMPARISON OF REPAIRS AND RELATED
LOST WORKING TIME FOR FOUR MAKES
OF CARS FOR TWO YEARS

Make	Number of Repairs	Repair Expense	Working Hours Lost*	Total Burden
SC-A	8	$234	40	$434
SC-B	8	230	40	430
SC-C	6	160	30	310
SC-D	6	175	30	325

*Based on hourly wage of $5
Source: Allied Distributors, Inc., Operating Records

As shown in Table III, SC-A has the best record for oil and gas economy with a per-mile cost of .01719 cents. SC-C with a cost of .01901 cents, is second; SC-B is third with .01964 cents; and SC-D is last with .02096 cents. Computed on the basis of 55,000 miles (the two-year mileage average for company cars), these costs mean a $174.35 margin per car for SC-A over SC-D, or $8,717.50

TABLE III
COST-PER-MILE ESTIMATE OF OPERATION

	SC-A	SC-B	SC-C	SC-D
Depreciation	$0.01590	$0.01583	$0.01527	$0.01538
Gas	0.01657	0.01852	0.01657	0.01852
Oil	0.00122	0.00122	0.00244	0.00244
Tires	0.00129	0.00093	0.00048	0.00035
Repairs	0.00414	0.00413	0.00301	0.00365
Miscellaneous	0.00246	0.00275	0.00214	0.00190
Total	$0.04158	$0.04338	$0.04001	$0.04224

Source: Allied Distributors, Inc., Operating Records

6

for the fleet of 50 cars. Compared with SC-C, there is
a margin per car of $67.10, or a fleet total of $3,355.
SC-B comparisons show a per car margin of $101.75, or a
fleet total of $5,087.50.

D. Cost Composite Favors SC-C

Consolidation of all the cost figures (see Table III)
shows SC-C to be the most economical make. Total cost
per mile for SC-C is .04001 cents, as compared with .04158
cents for SC-A, .04224 for SC-D, and .04338 for SC-B.
These figures take on more meaningful form when converted
to total fleet costs over the two-year period the cars will
be owned. As shown in Chart 1, a fleet of 50 SC-C's would
cost Allied a total of $110,027, which is $4,317 under the

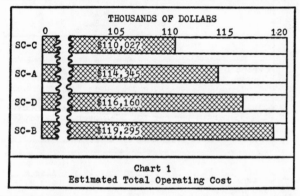

Chart 1
Estimated Total Operating Cost

$114,345 total cost of SC-A. SC-D, with a total cost of
$116,160, would cost $6,132 more than SC-C. SC-B, with
the highest total cost of $119,295, would cost $9,267
more than SC-C.

III. EVALUATION OF SAFETY FEATURES

Although costs receive major consideration in the selection of replacements, the safety features of each make
must also be analyzed. In fact, as salesmen spend a large

part of their time traveling and thus need maximum pro-
tection from hazards encountered in driving, the lowest
operating expense may be sacrificed in order to obtain
added safety features.

A. SC-D Is Best Equipped With Safety Devices

Only SC-D has as standard equipment all five of the extra
safety devices considered desirable by The Consumers
Safety Council. The SC-D is fully equipped with front
disc brakes, vacuum brake assist, adjustable seatbacks,
flow-through ventilation, and anti-glare mirror, as shown
in Table IV. The SC-D's braking system differs from that

TABLE IV LIST OF STANDARD SAFETY FEATURES				
FEATURE	SC-A	SC-B	SC-C	SC-D
Front Disc Brakes	Yes	No	Yes	Yes
Vacuum Brake Assist	No	No	No	Yes
Adjustable Seatback	No	No	No	Yes
Flow-through Ventilation	Yes	No	Yes	Yes
Anti-glare Mirror	No	No	No	Yes
Source: Road and Track				

of the SC-A's and SC-C's in that it provides vacuum assistance. The SC-B does not equip its cars with either
disc brakes or vacuum assistance.

SC-A and SC-C are tied in the field of safety features
with two out of the possible five shown in Table IV. The
SC-B, although offering three of these features as options,
does not provide any of the possible five.

Now that the Federal Government has legislated the basic
safety requirements, such as, seat belts, padded dash-
boards, collapsible steering column, and shatter-proof
windshields, the extra safety features of the SC-D are
even more welcome.

8

B. <u>Acceleration</u> <u>Adds</u> <u>Extra</u> <u>Safety</u> <u>to</u> SC-D

A life-saving factor that differs greatly among the four
makes is acceleration. It is important as a safety "on-
the-spot" need--something to have when in a pinch. Especially is it important in low-powered subcompact automobiles. When needed, acceleration should be available
in the safest car. It should never be depended on by a
driver to the extent of his taking chances because he
knows that it is available, but it must be included in
any brand comparison.

While SC-C's acceleration time from 0 to 30 miles per
hour is the fastest in the group, the SC-D leads in both
0 to 60 mph times and in the ¼ mile acceleration runs.
As shown in Chart 2, SC-C reached 30 mph .3 seconds sooner

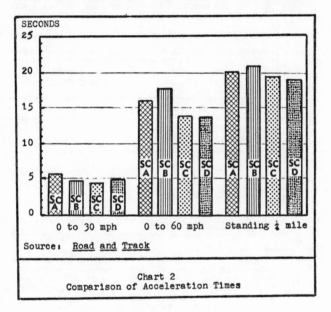

Source: <u>Road</u> <u>and</u> <u>Track</u>

Chart 2
Comparison of Acceleration Times

than SC-B, and .5 and 1.5 seconds sooner than SC-D and
SC-A, respectively. SC-D reached 60 mph .4 seconds sooner
than SC-C, which is not a very significant length of time.
The SC-D, however, achieved this same speed a full 3 seconds faster than SC-A, and 4.5 seconds sooner than SC-B.

C. Weight Distribution Is Best in SC-A and SC-C

Weight distribution affects not only the acceleration of
an automobile, but also the effectiveness of its brakes
and its handling abilities. The correct proportion of
weight on the rear wheels balances the car and in doing
so controls body movements in cornering and braking.
The problem is generally caused by the placement of the
engine in the front of the automobile. The arrangement
of the other essential heavy items at various spots on
the chassis results in the best distribution.

As shown in Table V, SC-A and SC-C are tied in this cate-

TABLE V
COMPARATIVE WEIGHT DISTRIBUTIONS,
BRAKING DISTANCES, AND CORNERING ABILITIES

	SC-A	SC-B	SC-C	SC-D
Distribution, rear, %	47	45	47	43
Braking, 80-0 mph, ft.	330	331	321	390
Brake fade, % increase in pedal effort	30	33	14	43
Control, panic stop	good	fair	excel	fair
Lateral acceleration, in g units	0.680	0.685	0.611	0.614
speed achieved, mph	32.0	32.1	30.2	30.3

Source: Road and Track

gory. Their 47 percent is near the 50 percent a 'tomo-
tive experts consider best. In contrast, SC-D carries
a relatively low proportion (43 percent) of its weight
on the rear wheels. This low proportion of weight is
not good from the standpoint of traction on slippery roads
that seem to be common throughout the Allied sales territory. The SC-B is between the two extremes with 45
percent of its weight on its rear wheels.

10

D. SC-C Has Best Braking Quality

At speeds of 80 miles per hour, SC-C stops in the shortest distance (321 feet); but SC-A (330 feet) and SC-B
(331 feet) are not far behind. SC-D is well back (390
feet). In tests simulating panic-stop situations, SC-C's
brakes also prove superior to the others, rank "excel-
lent" by test standards. On the same test scale, SC-A's
brakes rank "good" and SC-B's and SC-D's brakes rank
"fair." SC-C brakes also are more resistant to fade than
are the other three. In stops from 80 miles per hour,
all makes exhibit good braking control except SC-B. Its
stops are far less consistent than the others.

An over-all review of safety features shows SC-C to have
a very slight advantage over the other cars. Its brakes,
weight distribution, and stopping distance lead to this
conclusion. SC-A is second, scoring high in all categories except acceleration and standard safety features.
SC-D is third with the best acceleration but poor braking action. SC-B is last, having only scored highly in
cornering ability.

IV. RIDING COMFORT AND OVER-ALL CONSTRUCTION

Few things affect the day's work of a traveling salesman
more than the ride he gets in his car. Thus, the factors
of handling ease and general riding quality should be
considered in selecting his car. Somewhat related to
these factors are the over-all qualities of construction
of the cars in question.

A. SC-C Ranks First in Handling

The SC-C, with near perfect steering, is over-all best
handling car of the group. As shown in Table VI, SC-C
exceeds all of the other makes when values are assigned
to each category. SC-A, which is second in this area,
is quick and predictable in handling. During emergency
situation tests, however, it jarred and rocked severely
around bumpy corners. SC-D, while exhibiting normal
handling characteristics during routine driving, per-
formed miserably when subjected to emergency handling
tests. SC-B suffered from being knocked off course by
almost any small bump. When smoother roads were encountered, SC-B's handling was judged somewhat below average.

	Front seating	Rear seating	Ride light load	Ride full load	Handl-ing	Steering effort
TABLE VI						
COMPARATIVE COMFORT AND RIDE						
Excellent						
Good						SC-C
Fair-to-good	SC-C SC-A SC-D	SC-C	SC-A		SC-D SC-A	
Fair	SC-B		SC-C		SC-B	
Fair-to-poor		SC-D	SC-D	SC-C SC-D		
Poor		SC-A SC-B	SC-B	SC-B SC-A		
Low						
Low-to-moderate						SC-B SC-A SC-C
Moderate						SC-D

Source: Consumers Union of United States, Inc.

B. SC-C Gives Best Ride

While it is true that SC-A's ride has been judged superior to SC-C's when loaded lightly, SC-C comes out first
over-all because of the quickly deteriorating ride SC-A
exhibits when its load is increased. SC-C's superior
ride and directional stability are the best in the group
primarily because of its fully independent suspension.
A rarity in any front engined car, much less a car in
this price field, SC-C's front bucket seats are judged
fair-to-good in comfort--relatively high rating in economy car circles. As shown in Table VI SC-C's rear seat-
ing comfort is the best in the group.

C. SC-C Is Judged Most Durable

The SC-C is assembled with better-than-average care.
In fact, Consumer Research engineers have found only 16
minor defects in the car. In addition, the SC-C has a
better-than-average record for frequency of repairs.

12

SC-D, second in this category, has only 20 problems.
Some of these problems are judged to be serious, however.
For instance, in the tests run the starter refused to
disengage after a few hundred miles had accumulated on
the car. The car's ignition timing, idle mixture, and
idle speed were incorrectly set. An optically distorted
windshield and inside mirror were discovered. In spite
of all these defects, the SC-D ranks above SC-A and SC-B
on durability.

Clearly, SC-C leads in all categories of riding comfort
and over-all construction. It handles best. It gives
the best ride. And it has some definite construction
advantages over the other three.

V. RECOMMENDATION OF SC-C

Normally, this simulation cannot be merely a count of
rankings on the evaluations made, for the qualities carry
different weights. Cost, for example, is the major factor
in most such decisions. In this instance, however, weighting is not necessary for one automobile is the clear leader on all three of the bases used for evaluation. Thus,
it would lead in any arrangement of weights.

From the data presented, SC-C is the best buy when all
costs are considered. The total difference on a purchase
of 50 automobiles is a significant $5,300 over the second-
place brand. SC-C has a slight edge when safety features
are considered. And it is the superior car in handling
ease, ride quality, and construction. These facts point
clearly to the recommendation that Allied buy SC-C's this
year.

Appendix B

Illustration of a short report

In the following pages appears a short report written in the direct order (recommendation and summary first). As its introduction reviews the background facts of the problem, most of which are known to the immediate reader, the report apparently is designed for future reference. For reasons of convention in the accounting field, the writing style of the report is somewhat reserved and formal.

RECOMMENDATIONS FOR DEPRECIATING DELIVERY TRUCKS

BASED ON AN ANALYSIS OF THREE PLANS

PROPOSED FOR THE BAGGET LAUNDRY COMPANY

Submitted to

Mr. Ralph P. Bagget, President
Bagget Laundry Company
312 Dauphine Street
New Orleans, Louisiana 70102

Prepared by

Charles W. Brewington, C.P.A.
Brewington and Karnes, Certified Public Accountants
743 Beaux Avenue, New Orleans, Louisiana 70118

April 16, 197X

RECOMMENDATIONS FOR DEPRECIATING DELIVERY TRUCKS

BASED ON AN ANALYSIS OF THREE PLANS

PROPOSED FOR THE BAGGET LAUNDRY COMPANY

I. Recommendations and Summary of Analysis

The Reducing Charge method appears to be the best method to depreciate Bagget Laundry Company delivery trucks. The relative equality of cost allocation for depreciation and maintenance over the useful life of the trucks is the prime advantage under this method. Computation of depreciation charges is relatively simple by the Reducing Charge plan but not quite so simple as computation under the second best method considered.

The second best method considered is the Straight-Line depreciation plan. It is the simplest to compute of the plans considered, and it results in yearly charges equal to those under the Reducing Charge method. The unequal cost allocation resulting from increasing maintenance costs in successive years, however, is a disadvantage that far outweighs the method's ease of computation.

Third among the plans considered is the Service Hours method. This plan is not satisfactory for depreciating delivery trucks primarily because it combines a number of undesirable features. Prime among these is the complexity and cost of computing yearly charges under the plan. Also significant is the likelihood of poor cost allocation under this plan. An additional drawback is the possibility of variations in the estimates of the service life of company trucks.

II. Background of the Problem

Authorization of the Study. This report on depreciation methods for delivery trucks of the Bagget Laundry Company is submitted on April 16, 19X2, to Mr. Ralph P. Bagget, President of the Company. Authorization for this report was given orally by Mr. Bagget to Mr. Charles W. Brewington, Brewington and Karnes, Certified Public Accountants, on March 15, 19X2.

Statement of the Problem. Having decided to establish branch agencies, the Bagget Laundry Company has purchased delivery trucks to transport laundry back and forth from the central cleaning plant in downtown New Orleans. The problem is to select the most advantageous method to depreciate the trucks. The trucks have an original cost of $3750, a five-year life, and a trade-in value of $750.

Method of Solving the Problem. Study of Company records and a review of the authoritative writings on the subject have been used in seeking a reliable solution to the Bagget Laundry Company's problem. Alternative methods of depreciating delivery trucks have been selected through the experience and study of the writer. Conclusions are based on generally accepted business principles as set forth by experts in the field of depreciation.

2

<u>Steps in Analyzing the Problem</u>   The depreciation methods evaluated in this report are discussed in order of their rank as a solution to the problem. No attempt has been made to isolate the factors discussed under each method. Since each method contains fixed factors, a comparison of them directly would be meaningless, because they cannot be manipulated. The method of computation, amount of depreciation each year, and effect of maintenance costs are the factors to be considered. The Reducing Charge method will be discussed first.

III. <u>Marked Advantages of the Reducing Charge Method</u>

The Reducing Charge method, sometimes called the Sum-of-the-Digits method, is an application of a series of diminishing fractions to be applied over the life of the trucks. The fractions to be applied to the five-year life of the delivery trucks are computed by adding the sum of the years (the denominator) and relating this to the number of position of the year (the numerator). Each fraction is applied against the depreciable value of the trucks. Computation of the depreciable value is made by subtracting the trade-in value from the original cost. The depreciable value for the delivery trucks is $3000 ($3750 – $750).

This method results in larger depreciation costs for the early years, with subsequent decreases in the latter years. Since maintenance and repair costs can be expected to be higher in later years, however, this method provides a relatively stable charge for each year as shown in Table I.

	Table I		
	DEPRECIATION AND MAINTENANCE COSTS FOR DELIVERY TRUCKS OF BAGGET LAUNDRY FOR 19X0-19X4 USING REDUCING CHARGE DEPRECIATION		
End of Year	Depreciation	Maintenance	Sum
1	5/15 ($3000) = $1000	$ 50	$1050
2	4/15 ($3000) = 800	250	1050
3	3/15 ($3000) = 600	450	1050
4	2/15 ($3000) = 400	650	1050
5	1/15 ($3000) = 200	850	1050
	Totals $3000	$2250	$5250

However, since in actual practice the maintenance charges will not be exactly proportionate, the periodic charges shown will not be exactly the same.

The Reducing Charge method combines the most desirable combination of factors to depreciate the delivery trucks. The equalization of periodic charges is considered to be the prime factor. Although computation of this method is relatively easy, it is slightly more complicated than Straight-Line depreciation, which is the next method discussed.

198

3

IV. Runner-up Position of Straight-Line Method

Compared to the Reducing Charge method, Straight-Line depreciation is easy to compute. The depreciable value of each truck ($3000) is divided by the five-year life of the truck to arrive at an equal depreciation charge each year of $600.

Since the maintenance cost of operating the truck will increase in later years, however, this method will result in much greater periodic charges in the last years. As illustrated in Table II, the inequality of the periodic charges is the major disadvantage of this method. This method is very popular in the business world today, but where it is shown that maintenance costs will grow in later years, it is not usually recommended. The stand taken by many authorities is similar to the following:

> Straight-Line depreciation is the method most widely used in business today. It has the advantage of simplicity and under normal plant conditions offers a satisfactory method of cost allocation. For a plant to have normal conditions two factors must exist: (1) accumulation of properties over a period of years so that the total of depreciation and maintenance costs will be comparatively even, and (2) a relatively stable amount of earnings each year so that depreciation as a percentage of net income does not fluctuate widely.[1]

Table II

DEPRECIATION AND MAINTENANCE COSTS FOR DELIVERY TRUCKS OF BAGGET LAUNDRY FOR 19X0-19X4 USING STRAIGHT-LINE DEPRECIATION

End of Year	Depreciation	Maintenance	Sum
1	1/15 ($3000) = $ 600	$ 50	$ 650
2	1/15 ($3000) = 600	250	850
3	1/15 ($3000) = 600	450	1050
4	1/15 ($3000) = 600	650	1250
5	1/15 ($3000) = 600	850	1450
	Totals $3000	$2250	$5250

However, the trucks considered in this report have not been purchased over a period of years. Consequently, the Straight-Line method of depreciation will not result in equal periodic charges for maintenance and depreciation over a period of years. Although this method is used by many companies in preference to more complex means, it is selected as second choice for depreciating delivery trucks. The prime disadvantage cited is the unsatisfactory cost allocation it provides. The Service-Hours method which will be discussed next has this same disadvantage.

[1] Wilbur E. Karrenbrock and Harry Simons, Intermediate Accounting, South-Western Publishing Company, Cincinnati, Ohio, 1968, p.44.

4

V. Poor Rank of Service-Hours Depreciation

The Service-Hours method of depreciation combines the major disadvantages of the other ways discussed. It is based on the principle that a truck is bought for the direct hours of service that it will give. The estimated number of hours that a delivery truck can be used efficiently according to automotive engineers is one-hundred thousand miles. The depreciable cost ($3000) for each truck is allocated pro rata according to the number of service hours used.

The difficulty and expense of maintaining additional records of service hours is a major disadvantage of this method. The depreciation cost for the delivery trucks under this method will fluctuate widely between first and last years. It is reasonable to assume that as the trucks get older more time will be spent on maintenance. Consequently, the larger depreciation costs will occur in the initial years. As can be seen by Table III, the periodic charges for depreciation and maintenance hover between the two previously discussed methods.

The periodic charge for depreciation and maintenance increases in the later years of ownership. Another difficulty encountered is the possibility of a variance between estimated service hours and the actual service hours. The wide fluctuations possible make it impractical to use this method for depreciating the delivery trucks.

The difficulty of maintaining adequate records and increasing costs in the later years are the major disadvantages of this method. Since it combines the major disadvantages of both the Reducing Charge and Straight-Line methods it is not satisfactory for depreciating the delivery trucks.

Table III

DEPRECIATION AND MAINTENANCE COSTS FOR
DELIVERY TRUCKS OF BAGGET LAUNDRY FOR 19X0-19X4
USING SERVICE-HOURS DEPRECIATION

End of Year	Estimated Service-Hours	Depreciation	Maintenance	Sum
1	30,000	$ 900	$ 50	$ 950
2	25,000	750	250	1000
3	20,000	600	450	1050
4	15,000	450	650	1100
5	10,000	300	850	1150
	100,000	$3000	$2250	$5250

Appendix C

Illustration of a traditional
memorandum report

MEMORANDUM

the CROWELL COMPANY, inc.

To: Charles E. Groom   June 3, 19X6

From: Edmund S. Posner

Subject: Graff Lining Company's use of Kynar pipe lining

Following is the report you requested January 9 on the Graff
Lining Company's process of using Kynar for lining pipe. My
comments are based on my inspection of the facilities at the
Graff plant and my conversations with their engineers.

<u>Dimension limitations</u>

Graff's ability to line the smaller pipe sizes appears to be
limited. To date, the smallest diameter pipe they have lined
in 10-foot spool lengths is 2 inches. They believe they can
handle 1½-inch pipe in 10-foot spools, but they have not
attempted this size. They question their ability to handle
smaller pipe in 10-foot lengths.

This limitation, however, does not apply to fittings. They can
line 1½-inch and 1-inch fittings easily. Although they can
handle smaller sizes than these, they prefer to limit minimum
nipple size to 1 inch by 4 inches long.

Maximum spool dimensions for the coating process are best
explained by illustration:

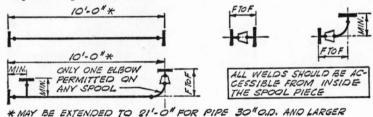

Graff corrects defects found. If the defect is small, they
correct by retouching with sprayer or brush. If the defect
is major, they remove all the coating by turning and reline
the pipe.

Recommendations for piping

Should we be interested in using their services, Graff
engineers made the following recommendations. First, they
recommend that we use forged steel fittings rather than cast
fittings. Cast fittings, they point out, have excessive porosity. They noted, though, that cast fittings can be used and
are less expensive. For large jobs, this factor could be significant.

Second, they suggest that we make all small connections, such as
those required for instruments, in a prescribed manner. This
manner is best described by diagram:

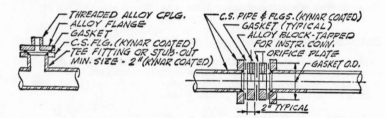

Graff engineers emphasized this point further by illustrating
a common form of small connections that will not work. Such
connections are most difficult to coat. Pinhole breaks are
likely to occur on them, and a pinhole break can cause the
entire coating to disbond. A typical unacceptable connection
is the following:

Preparation of pipe for lining

Graff requires that all pipe to be lined be ready for the coating process. Specifically, they require that all welds be ground smooth (to avoid pitting and assure penetration). Because welds are inaccessible in small pipe, they require forged tees in all piping smaller than 4 inches. In addition, they require that all attachments to the pipe (clips, base ells, etc.) be welded to the pipe prior to coating.

The lining procedure

The procedure Graff uses in lining the pipe begins with cleaning the pipe and inspecting it for cracked fittings, bad welds, etc. When necessary, they do minor retouching and grinding of welds. Then they apply the Kynar in three forms: primer, building, sealer. They apply the building coat in as many layers as is necessary to obtain a finished thickness of 25 mils. They oven bake each coat at a temperature and for a time determined by the phase of the coating and the piping material.

Inspection technique

Following the coating, Graff inspectors use a spark testing method to detect possible pin holes or other defects. This method is best explained by illustration:

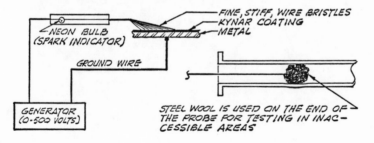

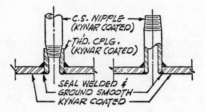

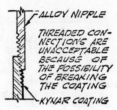

A third recommendation is that we establish handling procedures to protect the coated pipe. As the Kynar coating will chip, we would need to make certain that we protect all flange spaces. Also, we would need to be careful in shipping, handling, storing, and erecting the pipe.

Appendix D

Illustration of a letter report

January 28, 19X5

Board of Directors
National Society of Systems Engineers

Gentlemen:

Subject: Recommendation of hotel for 19X5 convention

Recommendation of the Lamont

The Lamont Hotel is my recommendation for our annual meeting in
December. My decision is based on the following summary of the
evidence I collected. First, the Lamont has a definite downtown
location advantage, and this is important to convention goers
and their wives. Second, accommodations, including meeting rooms
are adequate in both places, although the Blackwell's rooms are
more modern. Third, Lamont room costs are approximately 20%
lower than those at the Blackwell. The Lamont, however, would
charge $200 for a room for the assembly meeting. Although both
hotels are adequate, because of location and cost advantages the
Lamont appears to be the better choice from the members' viewpoint.

Origin and Plan of the Investigation

In investigating these two hotels, as was my charge from you at
our January 7th meeting, I collected information on what I believed to be the three major factors of consideration in the
problem. First is location. Second is adequacy of accommodations.
And third is cost. The following findings and evaluations form
the basis of my recommendation.

The Lamont's Favorable Downtown Location

The older of the two hotels, the Lamont is located in the heart
of the downtown business district. Thus it is convenient to the
area's two major department stores as well as the other downtown
shops. The Blackwell, on the other hand, is approximately nine
blocks from the major shopping area. Located in the periphery of

Board of Directors   -2-   January 28, 19X5

the business and residential area, it provides little location
advantage for those wanting to shop. It does, however, have
shops within its walls which provide virtually all of the guests'
normal needs. Because many members will bring wives, however,
the downtown location does give the Lamont an advantage.

Adequate Accommodations at Both Hotels

Both hotels can guarantee the 600 rooms we require. As the
Blackwell is only two years old, its rooms are more modern and
therefore more appealing. The 69-year-old Lamont, however, is
well preserved and comfortable. Its rooms are all in good repair,
and the equipment is modern.

The Blackwell has 11 small meeting rooms and the Lamont has 13.
All are adequate for our purposes. Both hotels can provide the
10 we need. For our general assembly meeting, the Lamont would
make available its Capri Ballroom, which can easily seat our
membership. It would also serve as the site of our inaugural
dinner. The assembly facilities at the Blackwell appear to be
somewhat crowded, although the management assures me that it can
hold 600. Pillars in the room, however, would make some seats undesirable. In spite of the limitations mentioned, both hotels
appear to have adequate facilities for our meeting.

Lower Costs at the Lamont

Both the Lamont and the Blackwell would provide nine rooms for
meetings on a complimentary basis. Both would provide complimentary suites for our president and our secretary. The Lamont,
however, would charge $200 for use of the room for the assembly
meeting. The Blackwell would provide this room without charge.

Convention rates at the Lamont are $18-$22 for singles, $20-$24
for double-bedded rooms, and $22-$26 for twin-bedded rooms.
Comparable rates at the Blackwell are $22-$25, $24-$28, and
$27-$35. Thus the savings at the Lamont would be approximately
20% per member(s).

Board of Directors   -3-   January 28, 19X5

Cost of the dinner selected would be $8.50 per person, including gratuities, at the Lamont. The Blackwell would meet this price if we would guarantee 600 plates. Otherwise, they would charge $9. Considering all of these figures, the total cost picture at the Lamont is the more favorable one.

Respectfully yours,

Willard K. Mitchell

Willard K. Mitchell
Executive Secretary

Appendix E

Illustration of an audit report in memorandum form

The long-form audit report which appears in the following pages is a special form of memorandum. Traditionally, this type is more conservatively written and more formal than are most memorandum reports. Although this illustration concerns a relatively small audit, it does illustrate the techniques and procedures of this specialized type.

To: William A. Karnes   Date: May 3, 1974

From: Auditing Department

Subject: Annual Audit, Spring Street Branch

Introduction

Following is the report on the annual audit of the Spring Street branch. Reflecting conditions existing at the close of business May 1, 1974, this review covers all accounts
other than Loans and Discounts. Specifically, these accounts were proofed:

Accounts Receivable	Savings
Cash Collateral	Suspense
Cash in Office	Series "E" Bonds
Collections	Tax Withheld
Christmas Club	Travelers Checks
Deferred Charges	

Condition of Accounts

All listing totals agreed with General Ledger and/or Branch Controls except for these:

            Cash in Office . . . . $1.17 short
            Tax Withheld . . . .   .21 short
            Travelers Checks . . . .   .97 short

Exceptions Noted

During the course of the examination the following exceptions were found:

Analysis. The branch had 163 unprofitable accounts at the time of the audit. Losses on
these accounts, as revealed by inspection of the Depositors Analysis Cards, ranged from
$7.31 to $176.36 for the year. The average loss per account was $17.21.

Proper deductions of service charges were not made in 73 instances in which the accounts
dropped below the minimum.

Bookkeeping. From a review of the regular checking accounts names were recorded of
customers who habitually write checks without sufficient covering funds. A list of 39 of
the worst offenders was submitted to Mr. Clement Ferguson.

A check of deposit tickets to the third and fourth regular checking ledgers revealed six accounts on which transit delays recorded on the deposit tickets were not correctly transferred to the ledger sheets.

During the preceding month on 17 different accounts the bookkeepers paid items against uncollected funds without getting proper approval.

Statements.   Five statements were held by the branch in excess of three months:

Account	Statement Dates
Curtis A. Hogan	Sept. through April
Carlton I. Breeding	Dec. through April
Alice Crezan	Nov. through April
Jarvis H. Hudson	Jan. through April
W.T. Petersen	Dec. through April

Paying and Receiving.   During the week of April 21-27, tellers failed to itemize currency denominations on large (over $100) cash deposits 23 times. Deposits were figured in error 32 times.

Savings.   Contrary to instructions given after the last audit, the control clerk has not maintained a record of errors made in savings passbooks.

The savings tellers have easy access to the inactive ledger cards and may record transactions on the cards while alone. When this condition was noted in the last report, the recommendation was made to set up a system of dual controls. This recommendation has not been followed.

Safe Deposit Rentals.   Rentals on 164 safe deposit boxes were in arrears. Although it was pointed out in the last report, this condition has grown worse during the past year. Numbers of boxes by years in arrears are as follows:

2 to 3 years	87
3 to 4 years	32
4 to 5 years	29
over 5 years	17
Total	165

Stop payments.   Signed stop payment orders were not received on three checks on which payment was stopped:

Account	Amount	Date of Stop Payment
Whelon Electric Company	$317.45	Feb. 7, 1973
George A. Bullock	37.50	April 1, 1973
Amos H. Kritzel	737.60	Dec. 3, 1973

212

Over and Short Account. A $23.72 difference between Tellers and Rack Department was recorded for April 22. On May 1 this difference remained uncorrected.

William P Bunting

William P. Bunting
Head, Auditing Department

Copies to:

W. F. Robertson
Cecil Ruston
W. W. Merrett

Index

213